The Last of His Mind

JOHN THORNDIKE

THE LAST

A Year in the Shadow of
ALZHEIMER'S

OF HIS MIND

Swallow Press   Athens, Ohio

Swallow Press / Ohio University Press, Athens, Ohio 45701
www.ohioswallow.com

© 2009 by John Thorndike
All rights reserved

To obtain permission to quote, reprint, or otherwise reproduce or
distribute material from Swallow Press / Ohio University Press
publications, please contact our rights and permissions department at
(740) 593-1154 or (740) 593-4536 (fax).

Printed in the United States of America
Swallow Press / Ohio University Press books are printed on acid-free
paper ⊗ ™

16 15 14 13 12 11 10 09   5 4 3 2 1

Library of Congress Cataloging-in-Publication Data
Thorndike, John.
 The last of his mind : a year in the shadow of Alzheimer's / John Thorndike.
   p. cm.
 ISBN 978-0-8040-1122-8 (hc : alk. paper)
 1. Thorndike, Joseph Jacobs, 1913– —Mental health. 2. Alzheimer's disease—
Patients—United States—Biography. 3. Editors—United States—Biography.
4. Authors, American—United States—Biography. I. Title.
 RC523.T575 2009
 362.196'8310092—dc22
 [B]

2009026118

For the radiant

Maximo Holst Thorndike

It was all leaving her in slow, imperceptible movements, like the tide when one's back is turned: everyone, everything she had known. So all of grief and happiness, far from being buried with one, vanished beforehand except for scattered pieces. She lived among forgotten episodes, unknown faces bereft of names, closed off from the very world she had created; that was how it came to be. But I must show nothing of that, she thought. Her children—she must not reveal it to them.

—*James Salter*

Acknowledgments

Thanks to my readers: Lois Gilbert, Sandy Weymouth, Janir Thorndike, Alan Thorndike, Ellen Thorndike, Bob Ginna, Natalie Goldberg, Eddie Lewis, Henry Shukman, Biddle and Idoline Duke, Paul Kafka-Gibbons, Ted Conover, Kathy Galt and Beth Kaufman.

Thanks to Harriet Guyon, Jack Lane and Marion Prendergast for the spirited and tender care they gave my father.

Thanks to the clear-sighted staff at Swallow Press. As a writer, I've never been treated better.

Thanks to the Ohio Arts Council for a 2007 Individual Excellence Award.

And thanks to three havens where writing came easier: The MacDowell Colony, The Virginia Center for the Creative Arts, and the Brooks Free Library of Harwich, Mass.

My father sleeps through the December afternoon. He has always resisted a nap, doesn't believe in them, yet now lies on top of his bed wearing a winter coat and his red fleece hat, snoring lightly. He's ninety-one. For an hour he doesn't move, his head tilted back against the pillow and his hands interlaced on his chest. Another hour and the light begins to fade outside. Finally I walk down the hall and tap on the doorjamb. I stand beside the bed, listening to his shallow breaths and watching his old face: his half-open mouth, the crust in the corners of his eyes, his patchy skin and tumultuous eyebrows.

December

"Dad? Do you want to wake up?"

He opens his good eye but doesn't say anything, just stares without moving. Outside, the long Vermont dusk is settling. Every Christmas Dad stays in this downstairs bedroom in my brother's house—but now his eye shifts from chair to window to door and back, making me wonder if he knows where he is.

After a couple of minutes he hunches himself up against the headboard. I try not to hurry him, because I'm always groggy myself after a long nap.

Resting in bed, he wears the old pair of slippers Al has given him, wide and brown and flattened at the heels. His feet are too swollen to fit into his shoes, and there's no chance this year that he will tramp across the meadow with the rest of us through six inches of new powder, as he did last Christmas.

When I turn on the table lamp with its cheerful yellow glow, he sits up and lowers his feet to the floor.

"What time is it?"

"Four-thirty," I say, reading off the digital clock on the table beside him.

"Is it night?"

"Almost."

His face is still lopsided from sleep, but both eyes are open. He takes off his hat and flexes his bony hands on the edge of the bed. I stand beside him until my brother walks in with some papers. Al has drawn up a couple of documents that will allow him to take over more of Dad's finances. Someone has to do this, because he can no longer keep up with them on his own. He wants to balance his own checkbook, but I've watched him try and he can't do it. He keeps records but they're scattered, and he'll sit at his dining room table for thirty or forty minutes trying to figure out what's wrong. Dates, names, money, math— it's all slipping away from him.

Al takes his time. He asks Dad if he's warm enough, if he'd like a glass of water, and gives him some time to finish waking up. But when he holds out one of the documents and explains how this will make things easier for all of us, Dad balks.

"I've given up too much already. I don't want to sign anything."

"All this one does," Al says, "is add my name to your bank account so I can make sure the bills get paid. It's still your money. There won't be any change for you at all."

"There'll be a big change. I won't be the one in charge anymore."

He doesn't look at us, but he knows what's going on. His mouth turns down as if we have already deceived him.

"Dad," I tell him, "you'll always be in charge. All you have to do is talk to Al and he'll do whatever you like."

We've never backed our father into a corner like this. We've asked him to stop driving and to accept help with his medications, but he's never had to sign anything. Al stands in front of him with pen and paper, but Dad shakes his head. He stares down at the floor, at the carpet, at his feet in their slippers. "I don't want to."

In the boxy silence that follows his refusal, I become aware of my patience, as if it's a commodity I'm spending. I don't know how much I have.

Al tries to explain. If checks bounce, he tells Dad, or if bills don't get paid, it's a problem for everyone. "I noticed this fall that some of your bills were overdue. It would really make things easier for us if you'd let me pay them."

Dad looks away. For a long time he doesn't say anything, and when he finally glances at us I think he's going to give in. Instead he says, "I want to go home."

He stares again at his feet. The windows are now black with night.

"I want to go home and take care of my own money and be in my own house."

"We'll be going back," I assure him. "I'm going to drive you back after Christmas."

"I want to go now."

How desolate this sounds. I am tied to him. I have brought him here and must take him back, and now have a bleak vision of the two of us sitting in his house on Christmas Eve on snowless Cape Cod, far from my brother and the rest of the family. We would eat some small dinner, sit in his living room and exchange a present. We would read. It makes me lonely just to think about it. Dad's two favorite times of year are the family reunion in August and Christmas at Al's in Vermont—yet now he wants to go home.

"I want to keep my house," he says.

"Your house is yours, Dad. We're not taking that away."

But he will not sign anything, not tonight. Al puts the papers back in a folder, and we reassure Dad that both house and money are his, and he can make all decisions about them. Slowly, by talking about our holiday plans, we bring him around. Al's two boys, Porter and Ted, will be here, some friends and neighbors will stop by, and we'll telephone our other brother, Joe Jr., and my son, Janir, who's spending Christmas with his wife's family. Dad stops talking about going home, but it's another hour before the stark look leaves his face, of someone hunted and trapped.

Over dinner he's still not his old self. He sits warily at the table with his hair uncombed and his eyes restless, looking at his food, then around the room. He turns to my sister-in-law and asks, "But where are the children?"

Al and I look at each other. We were the children, long ago. By now even our own children are adults.

"Tomorrow," Ellen assures Dad. "Some children will be coming over tomorrow."

This is true, but I'm sure my father is thinking about children young enough to be swept up in the mystery of Christmas. Back on Cape Cod, before we left his house, he showed me a pair of Christmas cards he'd bought, "one for my great-granddaughter and the other for my great-great-granddaughter." He has, in fact, only a granddaughter, my brother Joe's two-year-old Eliza. She's miracle enough, the first female born to our line since Aunt Annie, Dad's father's sister, in 1867.

My father is not the kind to take over a conversation, to assert himself or steer the talk his way. He has things to say about history and politics and economics, and he'll tell an occasional story, but he has to be drawn into it. During the meal the conversation swirls over his head, until I coax out of him a little vignette he once told me about Oliver Wendell Holmes.

"Well," Dad says, leaning forward, "I believe he was eighty-six." As he speaks he rests his palms on the white tablecloth. "He was out for a walk with an old friend in Washington when a woman passed them on the sidewalk. She was young and attractive and beautifully dressed, and she gave the two old gentlemen a smile as she passed by. 'Ah,' sighed Holmes to his friend, 'to be seventy again.'"

Dad's memory is irregular, and sometimes his language breaks down, but a little story like this flows out intact. It makes me smile, in its defiance of old age. This is the self-reliant father I've always known, with his dry humor and bank of anecdotes—not an old man who wakes confused and says he wants to abandon Christmas.

Usually after dinner he sits in the living room, perhaps with the rest of his wine, and at least listens in on the talk. But tonight, as soon as the plates are cleared, he thanks Ellen for the meal, says good night to the rest of us, and shuffles along the downstairs hallway, leaning on his cane. It pierces me, how old he looks, how even now he's passing out of our lives. His bedroom is carpeted and cheerful, but also the coldest in the house, and he keeps the door open in hopes of warmth. I watch him go into his room. I can see his bed through the open door and keep expecting him to climb into it, but for ten minutes he doesn't appear. He must be changing into his pajamas, I think, and I don't want to barge in on him. Twenty minutes and still no sign of him, so I walk down the hall and knock on the jamb.

He's sitting on the edge of a chair with his long underwear bunched around his ankles and his bare legs shaking. He's managed to get his pants off but not his socks, and these have stopped him from peeling off his long johns. He looks up at me, then down at his knees.

"I'm having a little trouble here."

His legs are pale and thin and nearly hairless. I kneel in front of him, feeling awkward, and pull off his socks, then his long underwear. I've never dressed or undressed him before.

We get his shirt off and his pajamas on, then a sweater, and he climbs into bed with his legs still shaking. I pull the blanket and quilt up to his chin, and when he's completely settled he says, "Thank you."

For the past few days he's been thanking me constantly. When I serve him a meal, when I bring him his coat, when I open a door for him, he thanks me. The formality of it has started to get on my nerves. He never says *Thanks* or *Great* or *Okay*, it's always a precise *Thank you*. It makes me feel like an attendant.

I'd like to sit down on the bed beside him, but I've never done anything like that, not since I was a child. I twitch his quilt around and ask, "Dad, how long do you think you'd have sat on that chair before giving me a call?"

"I daresay quite a while."

I laugh, but he doesn't. He has never liked to be helped, and only puts up with it when truly stumped.

In the muffled early light I come downstairs thinking of the Christmases of my childhood, when Al and I woke our parents with a string of Christmas bells sewn to a band of cloth. A wave of nostalgia runs through me. Where have those bells gone to? I'm sure Dad would remember them if I appeared at his door with them: their pure high tinkling sound. I look down the hall and see his empty bed.

I find him in his bathroom, where he has tried to get warm by taking a bath. The water now dribbling out of the faucet is barely tepid, and he's stuck in the smooth tub, unable to stand up in spite of the grab bars Al has installed. Once again he's shaking from the cold. I don't know how long he's been here, and when I ask he doesn't tell me.

"It's slippery," he explains, and waves me off when I reach out to help. "No. I can do it myself."

"Okay," I tell him coolly. "See if you can."

As soon as I say this I'm ashamed—but if he notices my tone he doesn't show it. He's already struggling to rise to his feet, but again can't manage it. After he settles back down, and without asking, I place one foot on the far side of the tub, slip my hands under his arms and lift him to his feet. How skinny he is. Deep pockets have formed below his collarbones, and the skin of his thighs is pleated like the gills of a mushroom. For the first time in decades he's completely naked in front of me, though he doesn't seem embarrassed about it or even conscious of the fact. He takes hold of a bar and makes the tricky step out of the tub, explaining what went wrong. "I got in too early," he says. "Something happened to the water."

As I help rub some heat into him with a towel I feel his new weakness, his vulnerability. He must know he's approaching the end of his life, but I want to protect him from this terrible fact. And I want to look after him. At least I do right now. I might not feel the same if I had to clean up his diapers—and that's where we're headed, I can see. At some point he'll be as helpless as a baby. But so far it's been no different from raising my son: the more I take care of him, the more I love him.

A few days later we drive back to Cape Cod with Christmas behind us and a long winter ahead. This past year was a difficult one for my father, for in the spring he was diagnosed with atrial fibrillation, and in July his longtime companion, Jane, died of cancer. Since her death he has lived alone in his house, determined to bring order to his books, notebooks, photos and file cabinets. I'm glad he still has the will for this, but he fights a losing battle. The real question is how long he can continue to live on his own. After Jane died his three sons—Joe Jr., Al, and I—all invited him to come and live with us, but he declined each offer. He doesn't want to live in Virginia or Vermont or Ohio. He wants to live at home, in the state he grew up in, near the ocean, in his own house. After all my recent visits I've left believing he could still manage on his own, but now I'm not so sure.

As we drive he turns oddly loquacious, and I draw him into a talk about his wartime travels as a correspondent for *Life*. I know he filed stories from Italy and North Africa, but I'm surprised when he mentions Australia.

"You never went to Australia, did you?"

"Well, yes."

"During the war?"

"And later. Your mother and I once drove there. We started out at the Bering Sea."

My hands are on the wheel. We're passing stands of pine and fir, whole forests of them, the nearby fields blanketed with snow, the road almost empty. *It's coming*, I think, with a small burst of panic. I glance at my father, but he looks completely compos mentis, staring tranquilly at the road ahead.

"You drove there," I say.

"It was a much longer trip in those days. We had to go down the coast, you see, and stay close to the water. But we ran into trouble around all the redwoods, and the road was washed out and we had to go inland to some little towns. I think it was near the Hearst Mansion. It was quite a long drive."

"What year was that, Dad?"

"Oh, that was in . . . That must have been . . ."

I have asked too specific a question. I'm sorry to have stumped him, because while the delusion about Australia is troubling, I love the rare mention of my mother, and how freely he's talking. Once interrupted he can't find his way back to the topic, nor can I lead him. I want to ask how it was possible to drive a car across the Pacific Ocean, but don't want to sound like I'm correcting him.

Though he's twisted the details, I think I know the germ of his story. In the late spring of 1942, when my mother was pregnant with me, and my father an associate editor at *Life*, my parents drove a great circle around the country, setting out from New York across the Midwest and the High Plains, over the mountains to Washington and down into California. Dad was looking for stories in those early months of the war. I'm not sure how the Bering Sea gets into it, unless it was the Japanese takeover of two islands in the Aleutians in June of that year—something my father, always the historian, might well remember. What strands are unraveling in my father's mind? Most of what he says sounds both calm and reasonable. I know he loved the California redwoods, and he has talked before about his visit to the Hearst Mansion, which he describes at length in his book *The Magnificent Builders*.

My father has written several books and edited many more, and writing is one of the interests we share. As young men we both loved to read, both went to Harvard, both had literary ambitions. But my father is an intellectual with a wide-ranging knowledge of history, art, archeology and architecture, and while I've written three books myself—a pair of novels and a memoir—I've spent as much time farming and building houses as I have writing.

My dad in his late twenties was an ambitious and confident young man who had started at *Life* straight out of college, and who eventually rose to be managing editor. I, at twenty-seven, dropped out of a PhD program in English and moved with my wife Clarisa to a farm in southern Chile, where we raised chickens and lived a peasant life. My academic career was over and my father's path left behind. There's always an element of rejection in such a move, and it couldn't have been easy on him, yet he wrote me steadily and sent whatever books I asked for, including a 1903 manual on traditional aviculture he found through a rare book search. He didn't ask how long I was going to stay in Chile.

On the Cape a surprising storm has dropped fifteen inches of snow on the ground, but Dad's driveway has been plowed. I help him into the cold house and crank up the furnace. It's exciting—but what a mess we left in our hurry to get out last week. Mostly it's the accretion of old newspapers and mail, of cards and magazines and catalogs, and of Dad's many notes. His three Christmas lists still lie on the dining room table, all in a shattered handwriting: Errands, Presents, and Christmas Cards.

Dad has made lists and notes for years, for decades, and sees no reason to throw any of them away. He writes on legal pads, in notebooks, and most often on three-by-five cards, which now spill across tables and shelves and his two desks. The cards, many hundreds of them, list telephone numbers, appointments and reminders. Some have quotations as well, though he's more apt to set those down in a notebook, along with his outlines and research notes. There are notebooks here from when he was writing his last book, *The Coast*, an exploration of the Atlantic coastline—and others that go back seventy years, from when he worked on the *Harvard Crimson*, or even further, to high school, with quotes from Gibbon, Toynbee and Virgil. They are the endless, restless work of the mind.

Last fall, as Dad's memory started to fail, he began to write daily reminders to himself. He recorded, on an undated three-by-five card that now lies on the dining room table, "Doctor's appointment tomorrow." He set down many times what I guess to be the current date, one to a card. He wrote "Harriet came," and "I've had my medications," and "Blood test tomorrow." One card says, "I've eaten breakfast."

My father, once so knowledgeable about the history of Western civilization, is now trying to keep track of what meals he has eaten. I pore over the cards. Half of them I can't read at all, his handwriting has become so shaky. I had planned, after driving him to the Cape, to head back to Ohio—but his notes dismay me, and I worry about those times over Christmas when he seemed so bewildered. I decide to settle in for a few days, and go to work on the papers strewn over his dining room table and his desks. Slowly, when he's not watching, I sort through the cards and toss most of them. I inspect the first few hundred, but can't always tell what I'm throwing away.

After the cards, I take on the piles of old magazines and catalogs. And his junk mail, diligently saved for months or years: the many requests from the March of Dimes, the Smile Train and the ACLU, the Natural Resources Defense Council, Lighthouse International, the St. Labre Indian School and People for the Ethical Treatment of Animals, won't you help? There are easily three hundred of these petitions, and one after another they go into the trash. Dad has told me to save them, but I don't. Though he can no longer balance his checkbook, I'm afraid he could still write checks.

I'm aware of my transgressions, of imposing my will on my father's house and habits. Even though I'm still only visiting, the chaos of the place unnerves me. It's too clear a reflection of the growing disorder of his mind.

A couple of days after our return he wants to see the suitcase he took to Vermont. I've stored it upstairs but bring it down for him to inspect. It's empty, as I assured him it would be.

"I'm missing some things," he says. "We must have left them at Alan's."

"You mean clothes?"

"And other things."

"What things?"

He doesn't answer.

I tell him I'll look around for them, or I can call Al and he'll send them down. "What is it that's missing?"

The frustration on his face is clear. "They're . . . those things," he says. But he can't name them.

All his life my father has been good with words. He loves the English language, and for a couple of years was head of the Usage Panel of the *American Heritage Dictionary*. But now he's losing his nouns, and he hates it. Of course he's been losing proper nouns for years, the way we all do. He can forget the street I grew up on, or the name of someone he's known since college—but now he's begun to blank out on common nouns as well, words like *chimney* or *swan* or *couch*. After dinner he asks me to replace "the . . . the . . . there, on the table." He can't find the word, but points to the lamp until I figure it out: the *lightbulb*.

"We've got plenty," I say and go off to find one. How chipper I can sound. But underneath I'm as worried about what's happening as he is.

Last summer, when my father started having trouble keeping track of his medications, we hired a retired nurse, Harriet Guyon, to stop in once a day, pour his meds and keep an eye on him. She's been a godsend, and even my father has adjusted to her. At first he hated the idea of anyone coming into his house, and announced he wanted nothing to do with her. He disliked her, he didn't need her, he was getting along fine on his own. But soon she won him over. After a week he felt neutral about her, and within a month she'd become indispensable to him.

Still, the time is going to come when he'll need more care. If he's going to stay in his disordered house, someone will have to live with him, and Harriet can't do that. Neither can my brothers.

Al is married and has a small-town law practice. Joe's job as a tax analyst and historian is more flexible, but he's also married and has a two-year-old daughter. I remember when my son was two, how absorbed I was in raising him.

In her last years my grandmother was looked after by a distant cousin, and I think Dad believes that at some point an elderly woman like his great-aunt Eleanor will materialize to take care of him. But there is no busty and cheerful Aunt Eleanor, there's only me—or only *I*, as my father would say—and I'm still holding back. I've had a good Christmas, but now I'm ready to go home. I don't want to give up my life any more than my brothers do. I have a hundred friends in Athens, Ohio, a house by a creek, a deer-proof garden with an eight-foot-high fence, and a part-time business renting out the houses I've built in the last seven years. I try to balance this against my dad's needs and my brother's lives, and there is no balance.

In spite of the jumble of the house, I love how my father's history is stored all through it. On bookshelves, in his desk drawers, in oversized file cabinets, in cardboard boxes and old suitcases, anywhere I look I find papers and photographs and notebooks. Dad doesn't reminisce much about his past— hardly ever—but the record isn't hidden, and over the years I've wandered through it, starting with his youth in Peabody, Mass, north of Boston.

His ambition and literary bent must have been clear to everyone by the time he graduated from Peabody High. He was valedictorian of his class and an editor of both school magazines, for which he wrote some earnest editorials. In one, he castigated his classmates for bad manners: "Most of us," he wrote, "do not know Emily Post from Caelano the Harpy." In another he urged his readers to do more than eat, drink and be merry, because "There is nothing like getting a head start on the other guy."

In the fall of 1930, a difficult year for the nation, Joe Thorndike entered Harvard on a partial scholarship. Money was on everyone's mind, and like the majority of his class he majored in economics. "My goal," he once told me, "was to make a million dollars before I was twenty-five. If you couldn't do it when you were still young, it wasn't worth it."

After four straight years of As at Peabody High, his early grades at Harvard were mediocre: C in German, C in Geology, B in History. This was because he was already spending forty hours a week at the *Crimson*, the university's daily newspaper. He wrote steadily as a freshman and sophomore, was appointed managing editor his junior year and president his senior. Each year the Depression grew deeper, and his goal of earning a million dollars took a back seat to journalism, a field where he could make some headway.

In June 1934, the day after his last Harvard final, he moved to New York, skipping his graduation ceremonies so he could start a job. He had wrangled a tryout at Henry Luce's *Time*, and after a month Luce hired him. He wrote movie reviews, then People and Education articles. He wrote some financial pieces for *Fortune*, where he met James Agee and Archibald MacLeish. Dad was something of a protégé of Luce's, and in 1935 joined a small team under Dan Longwell, who spearheaded Luce's plan to start a picture magazine. Both Longwell and my father plumbed the mind of an exiled editor, Kurt Korff, who had run a German picture magazine called the *Berliner Illustrirte Zeitung*, and who knew more about photo choice and layout than anyone in New York. The nature of the new magazine was endlessly debated, and so was its name: Luce originally planned to call it *Dime*, as it was going to sell for ten cents. By the time *Life*'s first issue came out in the fall of 1936, Joe Thorndike, at the age of twenty-three, was the magazine's youngest associate editor.

He had been at *Life* for only three years when my mother, Virginia, came to work for the magazine. Dad clearly had his eye on her, because when a visiting documentary photographer asked whom he should use in his film, my father suggested her as "the most attractive girl on the staff." She was filmed at a desk as she sifted through some photos, and a few days later my parents had their first date, a drink at the fountain at Rockefeller Center.

They married a year later, in 1940. Dad once wrote a description of their wedding, and included a detail I had heard from her and passed on to him.

> We were married in the chapel of Riverside Church
> by a Unitarian minister who was wearing golf shoes
> under his robe and skipped all the stuff about two
> becoming one, advising us instead to keep our own
> individuality (Eat of the same food but not off the same
> plate, etc.). John says his mother was miffed because
> after the ceremony I suggested we stop for ice cream
> sticks at a Good Humor stand outside the chapel.

My father has never been a romantic. He's not exactly a pragmatist—he's too fond of ideas, of art and literature—but I can imagine him coming out of the chapel thinking *Well, now we're married*, and then, seeing the Good Humor cart, *Wouldn't it be nice to eat some ice cream?*

The way to the top at *Life* led through Henry Luce, and it helped if he liked you. It helped as well if his wife, the editor and playwright Clare Boothe Luce, liked both you and your wife. A gauge of one's status at Time Inc. was how often you were invited to the Luce mansion in Greenwich, Connecticut. My parents ate there numerous times, but their most notable meal at the long table was on Sunday afternoon, December 7, 1941, when twenty-two people—including some who thought the U.S. should go to England's help, and some who thought we should stay out of the war—sat down to a late luncheon. They were eating dessert when a telephone call was answered by the staff. A butler brought a message on a folded slip of paper and gave it to Clare, who read it, then tapped her spoon on a glass.

"All isolationists and appeasers, please listen. The Japanese have bombed Pearl Harbor."

Whenever my mother told this story she loved to point out how the biggest news of the century had been delivered not to the biggest newsman of the century, but to his wife.

My parents were married for twenty-three years. The marriage came to a bleak close, but the record of their early years looks hopeful. Here in Dad's house, in his voluminous files, are plenty of contact sheets, snapshots and enlargements showing a young couple at ease with each other. One photo shows them in 1940 during their first summer together, sharing a cottage with friends on the Connecticut shoreline, two years before I was born. My father looks handsome, and my mother slender and vibrant. I would have dated her in a heartbeat.

Joe and Virginia Thorndike with Bob and Patty Coughlan, at the Westport Country Playhouse, 1940

In other photos they board a ski train to North Conway, then stand jauntily on the slopes. They play croquet on our Connecticut lawn on the Fourth of July, my mother in shorts, gesturing, caught in midsentence. Oliver Jensen and James Parton ply their wooden mallets, while Fritz Kirkland arms a pipe bomb and his wife Sally lounges in an elegant dress. I'm drawn to my parents' shining years, their first ten or fifteen, when they and their friends were so young and spirited. Though I later turned my back on that world, now I can't look at it enough. I love their ease and confidence.

Last fall, while visiting my dad, I drove him down to Connecticut to see his old pal Oliver Jensen. Oliver and Joe go way back. They met at *Life* in the forties and later started two hardcover, ad-free magazines, *American Heritage* and *Horizon*. I hadn't seen Oliver in decades, but I remembered him from his many visits to our house when I was young. He was a big guy with a wide smile and an impish look. He liked kids but never had any of his own. He liked jokes, he liked women, he was married five times. He liked railroads and once bought one, a Connecticut spur that still operates nostalgic steam engine trips. But all that had passed by. Now Oliver lived in a nursing home, and as we turned off the interstate my father warned me, "He's not doing very well."

"Can he walk?"

"I don't think he can."

"And his mind?"

"Not so good, either."

Even after my father's warning it took me by surprise to find Oliver, that shining presence of a man, belted into a wheelchair. His hair, an inch and a half long, stood straight up from his scalp, just like before, only white. He had the same large head and broad smile.

"Look who's here," he said as we all shook hands. "Where have you two come from today?"

I think he knew my father, though probably not me. For fifteen minutes he was congenial and alert, as we talked about railroads and the house he lived in before he was brought here. Then his energy drained away. He drifted toward sleep, jerked awake, drifted off again. In midsentence his head bent forward, nodded, and he went silent. Sometimes a little drool gathered on his lower lip, and dropped.

When this happened my dad and I made conversation, or we waited until Oliver came around. Twice he woke up and asked again, "So, where have you two come from today?"

At times he made perfect sense. I'd brought along a copy of his first book, found on my father's shelves: *Carrier War*, written during his Pacific service in the navy and a bestseller in 1945. Oliver turned the book over in his hands with pleasure, though he didn't open it. "I had a lot of fun writing that one," he said. He also claimed to remember the wartime telegram he'd sent to my parents the day after I was born: *Congratulations on best production yet*, signed *Ensign Jensen*.

In the midst of our visit, for a quarter of an hour, a woman in another room screamed and fell silent, screamed and fell silent. She had the right to scream, a nurse told me later. It's the law. Unless a patient is a physical danger to others she may not be confined or restrained. If she moans she moans, and if she screams she screams. Oliver's room, like the entire home, was clean and bright, but those cries gave an air of bedlam to the place—even if Oliver didn't seem to hear them. My father showed no reaction to them either, save to lean in closer to the conversation. We continued our visit as if such howling were a commonplace, but I couldn't get past the sound. Someone was miserable, and no one could do anything about it.

After an hour and a half my father and I said good-bye to Oliver and made our way out of the building, past the same long-distance stares of the old women and men we had seen coming in, some solitary on their beds, others parked in wheelchairs at the sides of the corridor. Dad moved slowly. He had refused to bring in his cane, and I worried that he wouldn't be able to reach his car. I didn't offer him my arm, because I knew he didn't want to be helped. He made it across the asphalt on his own, opened his door, and lowered himself gingerly to the seat. After he pulled his legs inside, I closed the door and he slumped against it. He looked the way I felt, exhausted.

For ten minutes we drove in silence. Finally I said, "Pretty gruesome in there."

"Terrible."

"And Oliver's worse, isn't he?"

"He shouldn't be there."

My father hated that Oliver was trapped in that home. Oliver didn't like it himself, but his stepchildren had sold his house and a lawyer now had power of attorney over him. Only two years ago he'd lived in a large old house like my dad's, filled with books and magazines and the possessions dear to him. Now he slept in a room with a bed, a chair, two dressers and a television. All his books, even those he had written himself, had been given away or sold at auction.

After another five miles my father regained his posture. He sat upright on his seat and said, "Don't ever put me in a place like that."

That plea from my father never leaves me, and whenever Al or Joe Jr. talks about a nursing home I remember our visit to Oliver's. With each day it's getting harder to imagine leaving Dad alone in his house. Harriet comes over, visits with him in the living room, then joins me on the porch. She's a talkative, energetic and cheerful woman, but her face falls when I ask her what she thinks. She's been watching my father now for five months.

"He's so much more confused. He's worse than he was before Christmas."

Just talking about him makes Harriet cry. I'm in awe of people, usually women, who cry easily. I wish I could myself, but it rarely happens. Harriet assures me that she can step back in, that she can come over for several hours each day. But she doesn't think that's going to be enough. "I worry about him walking around on his own at night. I worry about him falling again. I worry about him cooking. Twice I came over and the oven was still on from the night before."

The evidence is building. I know what I should do, and that night, as if to close the deal, Dad shows me again how confused he can get. An hour after putting him to bed, I'm drifting off when I hear a faint call from downstairs. I dress quickly and bolt down the stairs to find him in his bathrobe, standing in the kitchen with his cane.

"I need some help here."

He leads me into the bathroom and tries to explain what's upsetting him. "I have to get this straightened out. It's not working at all. You see, I press *here*, but nothing happens."

He presses his cane to a spot on the worn linoleum floor, beside a set of built-in drawers. It seems to be a precise spot he's looking for, because he keeps adjusting the point of the cane and pressing down on it.

"What's supposed to happen, Dad?"

"The drawer should open."

He taps the bottom drawer with his cane, and I kneel down and pull it out. Inside: old place mats, a package of vacuum bags, a bowl with a mounted nutcracker, some broken candles. I start picking things up, but he says, "No, no, that's not the right stuff. That's not supposed to be in there. If I can open this, those things will be gone. They don't belong there."

I start with logic. "Dad, I don't see how tapping with your cane could open a drawer."

"I have to press it," he says. "It has always worked in the past."

"You've opened this drawer with your cane?"

"I can't find the spot on the floor."

"Maybe you should be using your four-point cane—it would cover more ground."

I'm trying to be funny, but he ignores this. "I just need some help here," he says.

I study his face, seeing the trouble in it, the lines, the splotchy skin and furrowed brow. What's he worried about? What's wrong with the stuff in the drawers?

We struggle with it for another five minutes, but don't solve anything. What's really going on doesn't occur to me until I go back upstairs and lie down on my bed in the dark. The drawer is a sideline: what matters is that he has asked for my help. My father never asks for anything, and now he has. No matter that he wants to stay in his house, he would never ask me to move in with him. Instead, he'd doggedly make do on his own until disaster overwhelmed him. But this drawer that won't open gives him cover. It stands, I think, for all the other help he'll need if he's to remain in his house—which is what he wants most in life.

The next day I call Al, then Joe, and describe Dad's attempt to open the drawer with his cane. I tell them I'm torn, but I have to stay here. I thought I could put it off until later, until the spring at least, but now the time has come. I tell them that sometimes I lie in bed at night and think about those bedlam cries from the woman at Oliver's nursing home. I tell them I'm going to drive back to Ohio, pick up my computer and some clothes and tools, find someone to look after my rentals and their inevitable emergencies, and return to Dad's house. I don't tell them I feel like I'm stepping off the face of a cliff.

Both my brothers are enormously relieved, and thank me profusely. "But can you really do this?" Al asks.

"Sure," I tell him. I'm aware of sounding like Dad, who never complains about anything.

"How long? What if he lives for years?"

"I can't think about that. I'll come for now. After that—we'll see what happens."

I don't want to promise I'll stay here until the end. I can't imagine the end. After I get off the phone with Al, I arrange with Harriet to come over while I'm gone, every day, and I line up someone else to stop by in the evenings. Mostly, Dad will be on his own. He tells me not to worry, that he can take care of himself. But that's the whole point: I don't think he can.

On the morning of my drive I wake him at five o'clock. In past years he's always gotten up for my departures no matter the hour, but this time he remains in bed, looking frail and unsure. He lies back on the pillow wearing the red fleece hat he now sleeps in. I crouch beside him and put a hand on his chest, then take his head between my palms and all but kiss him. These unheard-of acts are coming easier. Fearing there's a chance I might never see him again, I blurt out, "Dad, you have been the greatest father."

"Well," he says. For half a minute we say nothing more. Then he asks, "When is it again that you're coming back?"

"In six days," I tell him. "Six and a half days. I'll be back next Monday."

"Write that down for me, would you?"

"I've pinned it to the bulletin board," I tell him, and bring in the sheet of paper so he can look at it. "Harriet can always call me, and I'll check in every couple of days." Dad can still talk on the phone, but making long-distance calls is confusing to him, even with the speed dial.

"And who is it who's coming today?"

"Harriet comes around noon, and Bob will stop by after dinner."

"And what day was that, when you'll be back?

"Next Monday. Less than a week from today."

Slowly, his face relaxes. It's an act of will, I know. He's still confused but lets it go. "Please drive carefully," he says.

Ten minutes after I get into my car it starts to rain. I hate driving in the rain and dark, but eventually the skies lighten, the rain eases to a drizzle, and I'm launched on the fifteen-hour drive I've made many times before. Halfway through it, out among the farmlands and ridges of Pennsylvania, my neck and back start to tighten up. The drizzle continues, and the wiper arms are squeaking. I stop to spray them with silicone, but the maddening squeal continues.

It isn't true what I said, that Dad has been the greatest father. He's been good, he's been great in many ways—yet there's a coolness to him, a restraint that can drive me crazy. He can't be emotional or affectionate. This seemed normal when I was growing up: weren't all fathers the same? But looking back as an adult, I see how much warmth I didn't get from him, and how much I needed. Not much has changed in all these years. He'll talk about the rise and fall of nations, about the Spanish Inquisition or the Age of Exploration, about Hamilton's tariffs or our failure to protect the coastal wetlands. All interesting—but what I most want to hear is how he feels. How he feels about my mother, how he felt about her when they married, how she felt about him and what went wrong in their marriage.

He won't talk about my mother, or about his second wife Margery, or about Jane, his companion of twenty-eight years who died last summer. He doesn't mention their names. If I have him trapped in the car and start asking him questions, he'll answer politely, as if I were an acquaintance.

My mother died more than thirty years ago, awash in depression, drugs and alcohol, only a decade after her divorce from my father. There was plenty of anguish all around, but I've never been able to talk to Dad about it. Under duress he'll answer the most basic questions, but he won't reminisce about the good times or analyze the bad. Almost everything in our family history is off limits. This can make me want to scream, but if I show my exasperation he pulls back into silence.

If my mother were alive, I think I'd be talking to her about everything. Certainly we'd talk about how hard it was for her to live with someone so reticent, someone who shrank from all emotion. This is a difficult quality in a father, and even more so in a husband.

I remember that early conundrum: if my house were on fire and I could save only one of my parents, which would I choose? This is a cruel question one child asks another, and when I was a boy there was no answer to it. But later, as an adult, I knew I would choose my mother. We have the same dark skin and hair, the same full lips, the same love of warmth and water. Her sensual nature runs in my blood in equal measure with my father's restraint—and as a young man restraint didn't interest me. I had plenty of that and wanted the other. I was like her, I knew. We both wanted to talk, to tell secrets, to dance, to caress someone. In the last thirty years I've thought many times that for me, the wrong parent died.

It's still raining, and my back is even stiffer. On the long pull through West Virginia I wonder if I'm going to be able to manage my rentals from a distance, and try to figure out how much I should be paid to look after my father. I'm going to be paid, that much is decided. "Either we pay you or we pay someone else," Al has told me. It will all come out of Dad's account, over which we now have full control, after he gave in and signed the papers.

Five hundred a week, I think. There won't be that much work, but I'll be on call every day of the month with almost no life of my own. I keep driving through the rain. I drive and drive, until I think five hundred is too little, it should be seven-fifty. The rain beats down, dusk comes, and I finish the trip as I started it, in the dark.

In Athens I have gravel to haul, a storm door to repair, a dozen other rental details to look after. I offer my house to Billy Renz, and he agrees to move in and keep an eye on the properties while I'm gone. I can't tell him how long that will be.

When I call my father he tells me, after I squeeze him a little, that he doesn't know what day or what time it is. He's not sure if he ate dinner, and can't remember if anyone came over.

I call Harriet, who assures me that both she and Bob have been there, and that my father has had both lunch and dinner. "But he's really confused. He can't figure out when you're coming back, no matter how many times I tell him."

I have two more days in Athens. I go out to dinner with friends, spend some cozy hours in my house with the wood stove burning, and pack my car. On my last night I get a call from Lois Gilbert, my old editing and writing pal from Santa Fe. When I tell her the news she says, "John, don't do it. It's a brutal job."

January

"I just spent two weeks with him and it wasn't that hard."

"Wait until he starts dying and you're trapped there."

"He's not dying. He's just confused and can't live alone anymore."

"He's going to die, and it'll be miserable. I cleaned my father's ass for three weeks while he bled to death out of it. My mother and I cleaned him, and my siblings kept their distance. What about your brothers?"

"They're pretty glad I'm stepping in."

"I'll bet they are."

"And I'm going to be paid. I think I can name my price."

"Well good! What is your price?"

I tell her I've settled on seven hundred and fifty a week.

"Don't be a fool, make it a thousand. Take everything you can get. You'll need it later when the resentment starts. You'll need it when you're there every weekend and your brothers are off on vacation. Or even when they're just going to work and making money, and you're paying someone to replace light-bulbs for some idiot tenant."

"I don't have any idiot tenants."

"You will."

While we talk I drift around my living room with the telephone headset on, looking at the photos on the wall: my father sitting at his desk at *Life*, my son Janir and I on a vacation years ago, wearing big Mexican hats and smiling after a shot of tequila. "Hey Lois, I've made up my mind. I'm moving in with my father. I'm leaving tomorrow."

"Then I guess it's too late." She pauses. "Off you go to be noble."

"Lois, you are a cruel friend."

She's not, of course, she's a great friend. How easygoing, how demure she seemed when I first met her—but it wasn't long before she began to pry at what I keep hidden, and to laugh at how I maintain my public image. And it's a deft little stab she has dealt me, because it's true, I like to be noble. I'll do the right thing, but I like it when people hear about it. Already I've run across friends in the health food store and at C&E Hardware and told them my plans. They nod, they say *That's great, you'll never regret it* and *It's so good you're doing this.* Already I've imagined how word will spread around town when I'm gone, how people will say, *Thorndike dropped everything to take care of his father.* The craving for respect and admiration: some might rise above it, but not me.

After my phone call with Lois I sit in my house and consider how less noble I'd have proved if my father had gone into a tailspin three or four years ago, when I was living with Nora and her son. I'll call her Nora, a beautiful and private woman who made me swear I'd never write about her. We had a five-year romance that didn't work out, but to which we gave our all, and I would not have abandoned our life together to keep my father out of some long-term care facility.

Following Nora, a bit too closely, I had a fling with the wonderfully perverse and inventive Tasia Bernie. I wouldn't have wanted to turn my back on her either—and all through that time I was building or remodeling houses, about one a year. I was always in the midst of a project and always in a financial crunch. Now, having worn out my right shoulder, I'm finished with heavy construction.

Sometimes I wonder if I'm getting too old for romance. I never think of myself as old, and still bound around my farm taking care of the land and the houses I've built. I play tennis every week, and have started hitting left-handed in volleyball—but I've also felt a creeping malaise about what I'm doing in life. This incipient depression rarely touched me when I was younger and raising Janir, a job I took over when he was three, as his mother's schizophrenia deepened. For fifteen years parenthood gave me a clear responsibility and focus. Janir and I spent almost all our days together until he left for college, something

I'd been looking forward to, but which stunned me. Of course I had left my own parents and gone off into the world—but it is to the *next* generation that we pour out our love. I've long since adjusted to living by myself, and Janir is doing fine. He's married and working and thirty-four years old, and we often talk or write. But unless I move to Colorado I'm only going to see him a few times a year, and I don't think I've ever completely gotten over how adrift I felt after he left, when I saw that our daily life together had come to an end.

These days I've been writing a novel, which absorbs me—though less in recent weeks, as I struggle with a plot gone awry. Occasionally, pondering my future, I've considered my old dreams and the paths I never took: I could move to Porto Seguro in Brazil and learn Portuguese, or to the south of France, where a friend and I could rebuild an old stone warehouse. Instead I have my houses to look after in Ohio, and now my father who needs help on Cape Cod. The call is simple, and having recently brushed up against depression, it's almost a relief to know that I'll be busy every day.

These are the years when our parents are dying. I make the trip back to the Cape in two days, stopping overnight at Sandy Weymouth's, whose mother died last summer after drifting into extreme senility. At the end she barely spoke and couldn't walk, because at ninety-four they'd amputated one of her legs.

"*Come on*, Mom," Sandy used to say to me while she was still alive, "isn't it about time to let go?" There was never enough intimacy between them, Sandy says, never enough connection. Yet their last years together were their best. She softened with old age, and on his visits Sandy often massaged her back and neck, or sometimes they simply stared at each other for ten or fifteen minutes, not a word said, a radiant look on her face.

"I helped her live, but I was ready for her to die," he tells me. "And now I'm ready for my father to go."

His father's kidneys are bad and he's on dialysis, but his mind is clear and he could live for years. Sandy visits him every week, or as often as his father wants. He takes him the raspberries he loves, and they share a meal and talk about the old days. Sometimes Sandy takes him out shopping, or just for a drive.

"I've done everything to prolong his life and nothing to hasten his death. My brothers have done the same—but what's the point anymore? He's ninety-six, he's alone, he's over in that expensive home eating up the money. That money would make an enormous difference to me now. He's had a hell of a long life, and I wish he'd let go of it."

It's an unseemly wish, for one's parents to die. But one of the reasons I'm friends with Sandy is that he's so honest with his feelings, especially the unseemly ones. Of course he does some prying about me and my father. "Why doesn't he just go into a nursing home? He's expecting a hell of a lot from you."

We're sitting on the platform in Sandy's house, a raised pair of king-size upholstered mattresses where he eats, sleeps and does Emotional Work—his practice of coaxing feelings to the surface and letting them rip.

"He hates nursing homes," I say. I explain how my father doesn't want anything to do with assisted living, eldercare, Meals on Wheels, any of it. He'd hate to live with a bunch of old people he didn't know, and he's not interested in exercise classes or yoga in a chair or trips to the casino. He's interested in his family and friends and books and ideas. "Your parents *wanted* to move to that home," I tell Sandy. "They liked it because they were social and always had been. But my father isn't like that."

I'm apt to launch into a rant around Sandy when I sense he's going to prod me about how I feel, the grail being some cathartic outburst of emotion: fear or rage or shame. "My father," I say, "has taken care of me my whole life."

"Which makes you feel great about moving into his house."

"I didn't say I was elated about it. But I'm not seething, either."

"How do you feel about it right now?"

"Weymouth! I feel all right about it. I'm a little apprehensive, but I don't want to start shrieking about the whole thing."

He gives me a look.

"Okay, I know Emotional Work isn't just screaming."

EW is an endless topic for Weymouth. It's his daily practice and hope for the world, and screaming is just one catharsis of many. I could also cry or flail about or contort in silence, all of which would be good for me. Both Sandy and Lois think I should be crying more, raging more, maybe laughing more. They're probably right, given how much of my father is still in me.

Back on the Cape I move into one of the upstairs bedrooms. I've had some fears about disappearing into the pocket of my father's life, of being swallowed by his needs and routines, and each night I feel a ripple of alarm when I lie down on my bed's ancient horsehair mattress. I've been here two days, I've been here three days, and already it seems like years. *This is my bed. This will be my life as long as he lives.* Four days, five days—these are drops in an enormous bucket. Looking ahead, there's nothing but me and my father.

On a cloudy afternoon I drive Dad over to one of the town beaches. It's foggy at the shore, and the ocean almost invisible. A seagull flares for a landing, struts up and down on the sand, then lifts its head in a long spasmodic cry. Dad doesn't want to get out of the car, so I open the window to the salt smell and the small reverberation of waves knocking against the shore. I've been trying to get us to the ocean every day or two. Dad never says no when I suggest a trip, and so far he's never been the one to say it's time to go home. Today I'm determined to outwait him—but then he trumps me by going to sleep. It's so easy for him. I look over and he's gone: head back, eyes barely closed, his gaunt face drawn tighter around his teeth. His hair has turned white in the last couple of months. It was gray for decades, and now it's almost pure white.

I sit behind the wheel and wait. An hour-long nap is nothing to him, and I wish I'd brought a book. Finally I get out of the car and close the door, softly. My father sleeps on. I mash across the sand to the edge of the ocean, crouch and lift a handful of cold salty water to my face, then walk down the shore for a hundred feet. In the last five days this is as far from my father as I've gone. There he sits in the car, slumped back against his seat, with the keys hanging from the ignition. Someone could steal him, I think, an idea that makes me laugh. I walk even farther down the beach, until his car almost disappears in the fog, until I'm too far away to stop a kidnapper. Of course no one is going to steal this old man. They're more likely to see him sitting there with his mouth hanging open, think he's dead, and report him.

He wakes when I climb back into the car, and I suggest that if he's ready to go we could pick up some food on the way home.

"I think we should," he says.

I love my father's language, the New England formality of it.

The fog has penetrated inland, and with it the gulls. They sweep over the parking lot and perch on the supermarket roof, their plaintive cries filling the air. Here on the outer Cape, the ocean is never far away. I drop Dad at the door with his four-point cane and tell him he can go inside, I'll catch up with him after I park the car.

He stands at the curb. "No," he says, "I'll wait here."

My father is formal, soft-spoken and courteous. Also stubborn. It wouldn't occur to him to steer anyone else through life, and he doesn't expect to be steered.

Just getting to the bakery section and the frozen food aisles takes ten minutes, because Dad must pause and consider everything he sees along the way: the blood pressure machine, the column stand with bananas, the pharmaceutical counter, the chrome dispensers with five kinds of coffee. On my own I'm a speed shopper, striding past the elderly and the harried parents who wheel their kids around in carts that look like little trucks. Alone, I can make it in and out of the store in twenty minutes. But Dad's gait has become a shuffle, and no one in the supermarket moves slower than he does. He ponders his choices. I've forgotten the grocery list, but it doesn't matter, because these days Dad figures out what he needs by inspecting what's in front of him. It takes us an hour to get through the store, and by the time we approach the checkout I'm ready to take off running. *Let's go,* I want to scream, *let's get out of here.* And at that point Dad becomes the shopper I always try to avoid in a line, removing his items from the cart with slow precision, one by one. From behind the cart I lift out the milk and ice cream, trying not to let my impatience show.

"How you doing today?" the cashier asks as she scans our first item.

My father turns to her, interrupting his work, and says, "Very well, thank you. And you?" He's unfailingly polite to anyone who addresses him, anyone who helps him with a job, anyone he meets. He gives people his unhurried attention, which is probably one reason why everyone likes him. I like this in him myself.

As my father's memory grows worse, I wonder about my own. I've read books by people who recall complex episodes from when they were three or four, stories filled with dialogue and vivid detail. As for me, I think my earliest years were happy, and I don't remember much about them. More, though, after I turned seven: a blaze of lights on a Christmas tree in France, with actual candles clipped to the branches, and my brother pooping in a tub that same year when we were sharing a bath, the turds bobbing to the surface and making me jump out onto the cold floor. Was the floor cold? Was it slate the way I remember it? The original story or sensation has surely been reinforced and adjusted over the years, which is why I still have it. The brain has been at work, jostling the neurons and synaptic constellations that comprise a memory and keeping my recall up to date.

In the years that followed I didn't pay much attention to my parents' marriage. I was a kid on a bike, a kid in a rowboat, I was off building forts and shooting marbles at squirrels. Now that I'm older I'm fascinated by their marriage and their emotional lives, but most of it seems out of reach. My mother died years ago, and my father won't talk. How much, I wonder, did they know about *their* parents? One generation follows the next, and we learn so little from what could teach us so much, the intimate lives of those who came before us. To learn how families work we turn to novels, to biography and memoir. We explore someone else's house—while the rooms I want to know about are closed off.

My father's duties must seem never-ending to him. He's supposed to do the exercises shown to him by the physical therapist. He's supposed to dry between his toes and to drink eight cups of water a day. He's supposed to take his medications, on time, and to brush his teeth with the new rotary toothbrush, then brush again with a special fluoride toothpaste. He's supposed to eat healthy foods, and walk around the house more, and not settle into one position for too long. He's supposed to use his lift chair, the one he calls the Monstrosity, and put his feet up for some hours every day.

He doesn't like the chair, he doesn't like the exercises and he doesn't like to brush his teeth. He resists drinking water or almost any other liquid and pays no attention to the issue of healthy foods. In the morning I top off his cereal with half and half, and every night after dinner he eats a large bowl of coffee almond fudge ice cream. Who would deny him these treats? He's a frail old man and his prospects are thin. I make sure he takes his medications, and beyond that I try not to press him too hard.

In the afternoon we drive over to Brewster on the bay side of the Cape, to a little beach near the mouth of a creek and some marshlands. It's a bleak winter day with a biting wind, the usual collection of seagulls and some diving ducks. I'm glad that my father is so amenable to these small expeditions, because after a day of looking after him, of sitting around inside, I'm usually desperate to get out of the house. In front of us the waves toss in the wind. It's hard to believe that last year this massive bay froze all the way from Provincetown to Boston. I remind Dad of this, but he has no comment. I'm living with someone who rarely has anything to say.

But as we sit in the car with the motor running and the heat on, a woman pulls up in an SUV. She gets out and releases a pale Labrador from the back compartment.

"There's that woman who comes to the house sometimes," my father says. He must mean Harriet, because he adds, "She has a dog but she keeps him in her car."

Harriet does have a dog, but this woman and Harriet look nothing alike. I can see that my father is drawn to the Lab—and then the woman opens the side door and helps her small son scramble out, bundled in a fat little parka.

"*Oh,*" Dad says, "the child."

He leans forward in his seat, and his spirits lift. Mine too, just watching him. My father is drawn to both dogs and children, especially small children, the source of youth and enthusiasm. Plenty of life ahead in a young child. Old people Dad ignores.

He dressed himself this morning, always a slow process, and came out of the bathroom looking jaunty in his blue bathrobe and a red sweater. But he wasn't wearing his shirt. He'd put his sweater on directly over his bony little chest.

"Dad, you forgot your shirt."

"Oh," he said, looking down. "So I did."

Eight months ago Dad was still looking after his companion, Jane. *Companion* is not a word he would use—nor *lover, mate,* or *partner.*

"What do you call Jane?" I asked him years ago. "What word do you use?"

Looking up from some papers, he said in the mildest way, "I call her my great and good friend."

Though never married, they spent twenty-eight years together—longer than his twenty-three years with my mother and his ten with Margery, his second wife. Dad and Jane lived together about half the time, occasionally at his house but more often at hers in Connecticut. They went to Blue Hill, Maine, each July, and spent most of the winter in Jane's Florida condo.

Last winter she was too exhausted to make that trip, and gradually retired to her bed. Throughout the winter and spring Dad stayed at her house, cooking, running errands, climbing and descending the stairs to her bedroom. But he was ninety and growing wobbly himself. In April the doctors ran some tests on him and diagnosed atrial fibrillation, an irregular heartbeat associated, among other things, with congenital heart disease, high blood pressure and intense emotional turmoil. Its most dangerous effects are pooling blood and clots that can travel from the heart to the brain. The doctors put him on a blood thinner and a pair of heartbeat regulators, and told him to stay away from abrupt exercise.

He went on living with Jane until she died of cancer in July. Then he was alone. The day after she died I spoke to him by phone and found him shakier than I'd ever heard him. By the next day he'd recovered a little, and from then on didn't mention Jane. He would answer a question, but otherwise didn't talk about her. He'd done the same after my mother died in 1972.

Every day brings some new confusion. A week ago, after a long shower and shave, Dad walked out of the bathroom with his soggy incontinence underwear of the night before pulled up over his pants. Another morning he put both feet into one leg hole of a pair of Depends and remained in the bathroom for thirty minutes, unable to figure out what was wrong and unwilling to call for help. He can still speak logically in short bursts, but the jig is up when he has to put on his underwear. I've heard of such confusion in the elderly, but it's a shock to see this play out in my proper father.

After a silent confused day, Dad sits down at the dining room table before dinner and starts talking as coherently as a year ago. "This president," he tells me, "has no sense of economic reality. We cannot continue with this trade imbalance. No country can keep this up. No country ever has."

Yet only ninety minutes later he lies in his room with his sweater off and his shirt unbuttoned. He wants me to do something at the foot of the bed, but can't remember what it is—or perhaps he can't put it into words. When I spread his jacket over his chest he jerks his arms and says "*No no no.*" His eyes are wide open, he's bewildered and afraid, and doesn't look like my father at all. It hardly seems possible that only a month ago he was living on his own.

For twenty hours a blizzard has been howling across the Cape. At the exposed northeast corner of the house the snow is only five inches deep, but on the leeward side it's up to the bottom of the windows. The power went off before noon, and with the furnace out the temperature inside started dropping and has now fallen into the forties.

It's an old and drafty house. There's some insulation in the attic, but none in the walls. The house was built a hundred years ago for the widow of a surfman, one of six who lost their lives rowing out from the Monomoy station to save the crew of a stranded vessel. It was paid for by the U.S. Lighthouse Department, and is known locally as the Monomoy Disaster House. All in all it's a solid old place—though when I crawl around in the basement, applying plumbers' foil tape to the ductwork junctions, the sag of the floor timbers is evident. They are timbers, not milled wood, and in places the spans are sixteen feet. In most of the rooms the windows are original, with aluminum storm and screens added outside, nothing really airtight. It's a handsome house, painted yellow, but it could use some work. The original structure, with four small bedrooms upstairs, has been extended, in typical New England fashion, with a gabled addition that now holds the laundry and tool room, and a set of tiny stairs leading to a bedroom under the eaves. I've closed off those stairs, and the ones going up from the living room, in an attempt to hold onto what heat we still have.

By now I've dressed Dad in long underwear, pants, insulated ski pants, a shirt, a heavy sweater and a parka, plus hat and mittens. As skinny as he is, he often feels cold when the temperature inside drops to seventy-five. Now he's in bed, peering out gamely from under a quilt and a sleeping bag. Not a word of complaint from him, of course, but it could get a lot colder in here with the wind tearing the heat out of the house. I've been taping off the windows, we have candles and flashlights and plenty of food, and my goal is to keep my father at home. I'm worried about him, but like the feeling of adventure. Already it would take a town snowplow and a fire truck to get him out of here—and then they'd take him to the vocational school, where in a power outage last year the elderly slept on blankets on the concrete floor.

Besides, he's interested in this storm. "How cold is it now?" he asks me.

I check the outdoor thermometer. "Fifteen degrees."

"Lots of wind," he says.

He has always loved severe weather. When I was ten he took my brother and me to see the path of a tornado that had passed through Holyoke, Mass. Whenever a hurricane struck the Connecticut coast he wanted to stick it out in our house, and once, in the quiet eye of a storm, paddled me down the street in our canoe. He used to claim that when humans finally learned to control the weather, political factions would evolve into parties based on climate: sunshine parties, rain and high humidity parties, and so on. He, however, would be a voting member of a tiny minority, the Natural Disasters Party.

Me too.

Twenty-nine hours of relentless wind, three feet of snow, the worst winter storm on Cape Cod in a hundred years. But after our primitive dinner last night, the electric came back on and the laboring furnace gained ground against the cold.

I worry less these days about whether I can stick it out with my dad. I'm having a pretty good time. I've been here three weeks, I've been here four weeks.

Last summer when we moved Dad down to the TV room, I went through his upstairs medicine cabinet and dresser drawers, gathering up his old medications. I threw most of them out, but this afternoon, on the shelf in his downstairs closet, I found an old cloth bag with a surprise inside: a dozen yellow pharmacy bottles, all holding capsules of the sedative Nembutal. Three different doctors had prescribed the medication, and many bottles were labeled "30 capsules" and contained all thirty.

Marilyn Monroe took Nembutal on the day she died. As few as two grams can kill you, and alcohol adds to the efficiency. Dad's capsules are labeled 100 mg, so ten caps would be a gram. Thirty or forty caps would do in anyone, and he has more than three hundred.

More than once Dad has voiced an aversion to the travails of old age, and at one point was a member of the Hemlock Society. The pills date from 1997 to 2001, when he was entirely lucid, and he must have brought them down to his current bedroom sometime after we moved him: before that he wouldn't have kept them in the TV room, where his grandkids often lay around on the couch. The cloth bag has been in plain view at least since Christmas, and his hand passes within a foot of it every time he reaches in for a shirt or sweater. But I think he's forgotten whatever plans he had for the drug. Suicide is a project for someone younger—or someone with a better memory. I take the bag full of pills upstairs. I feel the same as my father about debilitating old age, and I'll be holding on to the Nembutals.

Later, with the pills tucked in my dresser drawer, I have to ask myself why I didn't leave them where they were. I can't be sure he doesn't remember them, and I don't want to ask him about them, because that would remind him that they exist. In principle, I don't believe in stopping him from taking his own life, but in practice that belief has fallen before a more primitive desire: I don't want him to die.

I still avoid the truth when my father asks when I'm going home. "Not in this weather," I tell him, or "Dad, I'm happy right here for now." These are evasions, they're lies, and I wonder if I'm being cowardly not to tell him I've come to stay. I wouldn't have to add, "until you die," though it would seem implied. By now it might relax him to know I'm going to stay and take care of him indefinitely, because day by day he's more dependent on me, and that must worry him. If only we could address the whole process of dying and how he feels about it. But this is my father, I might as well wish for a different parent. Or be a different son—one who'd talk about those Nembutals and about my plans to stay.

I think of Jane's daughter Catherine, the only one in that family who had the courage to tell her mother she was going to die. The tests had come back, the cancer had spread, it was too late for any more radiation or chemo. But according to Catherine, only she would tell her mother, "You're dying."

Admirable, I thought. At the same time, Catherine had her own agenda. She pushed her mother to face death, and to talk about it. She read her poems by Rumi, she rang singing bowls and read to her from the Tibetan Book of the Dead. And Jane responded—or so Catherine claimed. At the funeral service she announced that in the last weeks of her life, "Mother finally became the woman I always wanted her to be."

I shrank when I heard that. Yet now, my hopes for my father are not that different. I'd love it if he changed—if I could change him—into a garrulous old man filled with stories about my mother, their marriage and my childhood.

On the phone with the nurse of my father's general physician, I mention how Dad came out of the bathroom a couple of weeks ago wearing his underwear over his pants. *Dressing apraxia* they call this, and apparently it's a sign, because within a day we have an appointment with a neuropsychologist, Gerry Elovitz, to evaluate Dad's cognitive functions. Dr. Elovitz is a PhD, heads a memory center on the upper Cape, and makes house calls. This seems a miracle, and even before he arrives I'm inclined to like him. He pulls up in a high-riding four-wheel-drive pickup and steps out onto the snowy drive carrying a fat briefcase. He's a big outgoing guy with a brushy mustache and a strong handshake. We chat for a couple of minutes about the blizzard, then I escort him into the house.

"Doctor Elovitz, this is my father, Joe Thorndike."

"Call me Gerry, please." He reaches out and shakes my father's hand. "How you feeling today, Chief?"

"Pretty well," Dad says. "Getting along pretty well."

That's what he always says.

Gerry warms him up. "I'm here to help figure out how your memory's doing. I just want to ask you a few questions."

He's a charming guy, respectful and not too intrusive—but I recognize on my father's face the lowered eyelids of suspicion. I'm sure he can tell, as Gerry hangs his jacket on the back of a chair and opens his briefcase on the table, that there are going to be more than a few questions. Contained in his briefcase are the tools of his evaluation: the Brief Psychiatric Rating Scale, the Mini-Mental State Examination, the Geriatric Depression Scale, the Beck Anxiety Inventory, the Life Satisfaction Scale and the Clinical Dementia Rating Scale.

"Shall we get started?" Gerry asks.

"We might as well," my father says, trapped but game. Almost from the start he runs into trouble.

"Can you tell me what year this is, Mr. Thorndike?"

"It's two thousand and five."

"Can you tell me what day of the week it is?"

My father hesitates. His mouth pulls down and his face tightens. "Give me a minute," he says.

The psychologist waits for twenty seconds. Then, in a level voice, he asks the next question. "Can you tell me what season this is, Mr. Thorndike?"

"It's January."

"What do you call this? Is it winter, or spring, or summer, or fall?"

Through the windows we can all see the deep snow from last weekend's blizzard. But my father, under pressure and forced with a choice, gambles on "Summer." His answer is tallied, and the questions continue.

"Can you tell me, Mr. Thorndike, what floor of the house we're on?"

"We're on the first floor."

"I'm going to give you three words that I'd like you to remember later. Here they are: ball, flag, tree."

My father stares straight ahead as the test continues. It is a test, and he knows it. He fails to count backward from a hundred by sevens, and when Gerry asks him to spell *world* backward, he's slow to start.

"Backward?"

"Yes."

"D . . . w . . . o. . . ."

Gerry gives him plenty of time, but he can't do it.

"Can you tell me those three words that I asked you to remember?"

He can't.

"Take this paper in your right hand," Gerry says, "fold it, and put it on the floor." Dad focuses and does this correctly, though I can see his hesitation.

Then, "Read this and do what it says." Gerry hands him a paper that says *Close your eyes,* and my father, instead, opens them wider.

From a set of simple drawings Dad correctly identifies a tree, a flower, a bed, a house, a toothbrush and a volcano. Instead of mask, he says masquerade. When shown a picture of a watch he identifies it correctly—but when asked to draw a clock and put the hands at eleven, he can't do it. This doesn't surprise me, because for weeks he's been asking me what time it is, even when a clock is readily visible.

"Can you name for me, Mr. Thorndike, the last four presidents of the United States?"

My father is a student of history and politics, and for years was a daily reader of both the *New York Times* and the *Wall Street Journal*. But the only president he can come up with now is the current Bush. From the couch where I sit, I can see the turmoil growing on his face, the grimaces and gathered eyebrows. Here, publicly, everything he has feared about his mind and memory is being exposed.

"Mr. Thorndike, would you name all the animals you can think of."

"Dog. Cat." He's shutting down now. "Mouse. Rat." And that's the end of them.

"Can you name some fruits?"

None. He's breathing harder now, as if under stress. Finally he says, "Pear. Apple."

"How about vegetables?"

A long silence. "I'm confused here."

He's exhausted, and it doesn't help that the evaluation is being done in the late afternoon, the worst time of day for my father, as it is for many old people. He'd do better in the morning, I want to say. I want to defend him but sit quietly on the couch, as I've been asked not to interrupt.

Later Dad will refer to Dr. Elovitz as "the guy who shows how stupid I am."

When the questions are over, Dad hobbles into his bedroom and lies down. He's flattened, and immediately goes to sleep.

Gerry and I stand in the kitchen talking. He takes his time and doesn't rush off, as late as it is. He'll return in ten days for a second, shorter interview, but he can give me a tentative diagnosis now: my father has advanced second-stage dementia, most likely caused by Alzheimer's. He's also depressed. For the depression Gerry will recommend to Dad's physician that he prescribe Prozac or something similar, and for the dementia, Aricept, a drug that can help slow further memory loss. Nothing can reverse it.

"It's hard to set a time line," Gerry says, "and he'll have good days and bad. But in the end, if he lives long enough, he'll forget everything."

Later, I sit alone in the darkened house, slumped in Dad's chair. What a misery, this disease.

Most mornings my father still shaves, though he hasn't had a haircut in months. His eyebrows, certainly never trimmed in his life, look like miniature squirrels that have jumped onto his face, and his bad eye sometimes droops to a close. When I find him naked in the bathroom, standing in front of the mirror to shave, I see how bony he is, his arms like sticks and his legs withered. He's much shorter than he used to be. We were once exactly the same height, five nine and a half, but I've probably lost half an inch myself by now, and Dad must be under five six. His skin is droopy, especially behind, where his butt has almost completely disappeared. Just a few loose flaps of skin back there—though I haven't looked too closely.

They say the sexual organs are the last to lose their youthful form. This seems to be the case with my father as well, for the only part of his body that hasn't shriveled is his penis. There's a jolt: *his penis*. By writing about it I'm gearing up to the scary day when I'll be cleaning it. That and his withered butt, after he loses control of his bowels.

Returning from some cross-country skiing on the bike path, I find Dad in the kitchen staring at a large round unsliced loaf of bread I bought at the supermarket. I don't know how long he's been standing there, but it might have been quite a while: he can pause in front of the shelves in the bathroom and examine the deodorants and razors and aspirin for twenty minutes. Now he's staring at this lovely, unusual peasant loaf, which he has removed from its wrapping and set on the counter that extends into the middle of the room.

I take off my hat and gloves, and hang my coat in the closet. When I come back to the kitchen my father is still standing on the other side of the counter, in front of the bread. There's no knife in sight, or cutting board. Dad looks up at me, then down at the bread, then up again. He lifts his hands from his sides and rests them on the vinyl countertop, on either side of the loaf. I start to ask him if he needs some help, but don't. I ask him that too much. Instead I wait.

Finally he says, "Just what do I do with this?"

Evenings in my house when I was growing up. Both my parents came home late, after six, sometimes after seven, my father on the train from Grand Central, my mother driving back from school or some hospital. She had gone back to college, graduated from Barnard, spent four years in med school at NYU, then completed a demanding internship and residency in anesthesiology. Day to day I didn't feel her absence, because I had Nana. Nana was Imogene Graves, who worked for us for more than twenty years. Neither *nanny* nor *housekeeper* is a big enough word for her. She lived with us, went to France with us for six months, became a second mother to both Alan and me. She was a Negro, as we said then, and married to George Graves, a barber and manager of Sugar Ray Robinson's barbershop in Harlem. On weekends she either went into the city, or Graves came to stay with us.

Alan and John with Imogene Graves aboard the HMS Caronia, *1949*

On most nights Nana served Alan and me dinner in front of an early black-and-white television set in the dining room. We ate there happily, watching Flash Gordon and feeding pieces of dinner we didn't like to our dog, Bourbon. When Dad got home Alan and I would run up to him, eager to see what he'd brought us: a comic book or a Matchbox truck, perhaps an Eek-A-Freak squeeze toy. My mother would rise to his kiss on her cheek, and that was the affection between them. They ate together later at a small table in the living room, with candles and some wine. I never thought of it as strange that I didn't eat with my parents. I never thought anything about our life was strange, including the fact that my parents didn't hold hands, or sit arm in arm, or kiss at some random moment, or sleep in the same bed. Of course, I didn't see any of that happening with any other parents, so it all looked normal to me. That's probably what it was in suburban Connecticut: the norm. It's true that not every set of parents had twin beds—but on television they did.

I know my father responded to how attractive my mother was. I can tell from the photos he took of her, photos I grew up with and now find in his files. In them she stretches out in bed with her hair spilled over a pillow, or leans back against the Roman Coliseum with her eyes closed in the sunlight, or lies on a wooden deck in a two-piece, flare-skirted bathing suit, her thighs lifted by the black tire tube beneath her. She often looks sultry—yet what I saw when I was a boy, the essential message of my parents' bodies, was that one did not touch the other.

Why should I care about any of this? It's history. It's not how I've lived my life.

Though in fact, I lived that way for years. I had a strict schooling in decorum, in prudery, in a public life with no touch. I remember that wretched question we asked each other in high school, even college: *Do you believe in public display of affection?* I grew up in the Dark Ages! And what was truly off kilter at home wasn't the lack of PDA, it was that my mother, against her nature, had trained herself to live without it. She managed that for years, before everything went to flinders.

Patti came this afternoon, the "physical terrorist," as Dad calls her. His ideal day is one in which no one comes to the house, but he doesn't resist when Patti shows up to run him through his exercises. Today, I think, he's even a little enthusiastic, as she leads him to the sink and has him stand on his toes, then lift his feet to the side and back. He doesn't do as well when she asks him to sit down on a chair and stand up again, three times. He quickly grows short of breath, and after two rounds she stops him. He gives her a hangdog look, as if he's failed a test. His skin looks slack and mottled. His bad hand, the one with the bent little finger, flutters on and off his lap. Yet what I notice is how he lets this cheerful and energetic young woman put her hands on him. In their sessions she guides him, she slides her arm behind his back as she leads him to the sink and shows him how to stand. He may call her the physical terrorist, but I think he actually likes the attention. Perhaps it's easier for him because Patti is a woman, and also official. She's a therapist. This is something he must do for his health—she isn't just someone who wants to give him a hug.

These days when I meet or part from my father I embrace him, just as I hug my brothers and their wives. But this is an innovation that came in with the seventies. I think Dad still sees it as a kind of craziness that has swept the nation, and that he'd be happier with the old way, just shaking hands with everyone, his sons included. But by now the two of us have been catapulted into physical intimacy. Every day after his shower I dry his feet and toes. I get him into his underwear, then lift his pants up over his pale and hairless legs. I tuck in his shirt, zip up his fly and cinch his belt. During the day, or when we're saying good night, I sometimes take his arm, or rest my hand on his shoulder.

He, however, does not touch me. It's not that he shrinks away, but he never reaches out. If he's looking for support, his quivering fingers will always seek a grab bar or his walker or a shelf, rather than take hold of my arm. He seems to do this from purest instinct.

I imagine he learned this from his parents, who were born and grew up in the Victorian age. My grandfather, a Boston stockbroker, was industrious and formal. Every day of his adult life, as far as I can tell, he wore a three-piece suit, only slipping off the jacket on the warmest summer afternoons. He was a small man, shorter than his wife and perfectly gentle—though when I was a child his somber look sometimes spooked me. My grandmother was a schoolteacher, an actress in local plays and something of a journalist: her articles for the Peabody Women's Club fill a small album. The two of them were in their forties when my father was born, a late and only child, and their devotion to him is clear. The thousands of boring letters they sent him over the space of forty years are written on folded blue or ivory stationery, two or three pages of news from his mother, a page or two from his father. He called them that always, Mother and Father.

They called him Jay. He had a dog when he was young, Mickey, and for a while a flock of chickens. Never enough playmates up on Hog Hill, where they lived in a house with a wraparound porch and a view of the farmlands below. In the photos of my grandparents, on the porch or the lawn in front of it, they always stand apart, sometimes ten feet apart. They never touch, and they never show up in a photo with my father, who worked the camera. My grandparents liked some space between them, and my dad must have taken that in through his pores. Indeed, it must all have seemed unremarkable to him, as it did to me as a child. There wasn't much affection in his family, but plenty of devotion—and that was pretty much what I got from my own parents. The difference is that Dad seemed comfortable in such a world, whereas I had to break away, sometimes going wild with sex, drugs and rock and roll just to prove I was free of the constraints.

Only six months ago there weren't enough hours in the day for my father, and now there's almost nothing he wants to do. He gets up in the morning, shaves, showers and eats breakfast. Then he usually stays alert for a couple of hours, especially if the skies are clear and sunlight pours into the house. Then a nap, and Harriet comes over at one so I can go to the library. She gives Dad lunch, leaves at three, and I often find him asleep when I return.

Sometimes, revived after dinner, he wanders around the house reaching out to books and photos, old calendars, notebooks and maps. He picks them up, sometimes carries them around with him, and I think they stand in for his memories and his once vast knowledge. When I pull down the first volume of *Horizon* I find an article on world population by Julian Huxley, a manuscript page of Milton's *Paradise Lost,* and an article by the British traveler Freya Stark on Ephesus and its temple, one of the Seven Wonders of the World.

In the foreword to that volume my father wrote,

> History speaks to us often in riddles, in a Delphic
> voice. Yet it is clear that we in America today are
> the inheritors of many a great golden age, heirs
> to much of the glory that was Greece and the
> grandeur that was Rome, and to the strength
> of a little island off the coast of Europe which
> bestowed poetry, literature, manners, and certain
> explosive ideas of freedom on half the earth.

I love how he gives manners equal billing with poetry, literature and democracy. I wish I could ask Dad about that now and about those articles and their authors. But I had my chance for decades, and whenever I came for a visit I was too wrapped up in tennis with Al, or croquet with my son, or some novel I was reading, to slow down and listen to what my father had to say about culture and history.

When I spoke to Gerry Elovitz after Dad's evaluation, he urged me to investigate some local nursing homes. Like my brothers, he assumed that sooner or later I'd find it too difficult to look after my father at home, and we'd have to move him. This may yet be true. I'm not blind to the hardships of taking care of someone who can't walk, who can't shower or dress or feed himself. My goal is still to keep Dad at home—but to check out the options, I called one of the places Dr. Elovitz had recommended, a nursing home with a dementia unit.

As I sat in the lobby, waiting for the admissions director, I listened in on a couple seated close by. The woman leaned forward, protectively, I thought, toward the man, who sat in a wheelchair. His left foot dragged on the floor, but otherwise he looked alert. I struggled to hear what he was saying but couldn't, as he was facing partly away from me. The woman was trying to stay calm.

February

"Don't say that. Keep your voice down."

Then, "That's terrible. Stop that, just stop it."

"You are, you're talking too loud. And you don't mean that. Don't say that."

"No, don't say that. Don't talk so loud."

All my sympathies lay with the old guy. He'd probably been putting up with this for decades, and now that he was trapped in a wheelchair his wife could treat him like a four-year-old: Behave yourself, don't talk so loud, be polite around other people.

But the man did not clam up, as a child might. He went on in his calm and unbowed tone. It was the woman who was agitated. Then I heard her say, "That's terrible. You've never had a prejudiced bone in your body."

Oh.

Several attendants had passed through the lobby, some white, some black, some of them Cape Verdeans speaking Portuguese. In an instant my allegiance switched to the embarrassed woman, and I wanted to shut her husband up. I've read how dementia patients with no history of overt prejudice can start talking like racists. Polite and decent old men can shrivel your heart. And I didn't want the attendants and nurses and doctors to listen to this. I didn't want some young black nurse, after hearing this wasted old guy spout off about niggers—that's the word I imagined him using—think the obvious, that the veneer had cracked, and the truth of how he'd felt all along was now spilling out.

I've heard stories of elderly men or women who physically attack the spouses they have loved for decades. We may partially excuse them, because their minds are giving way. Maybe I should excuse this old guy's racial comments and dismiss them as pure dementia—but I don't ever want my father to talk like that.

Katie came out to the lobby, an attractive young woman fifty years the junior of most of her charges. I liked her because she didn't pitch the place. She gave me a tour, talked about the patients and their needs, and let me judge for myself. The home was cheerful and clean, much like Oliver Jensen's. There were activity and rehab rooms, and a large carpeted dining room. I found it depressing that there was almost nowhere to walk around outside—but then, how often would they let my father out of the locked dementia wing? Which is where he would go by the time I could no longer look after him at home.

Katie punched us in. A faint smell of urine hung in the corridors, but perhaps that was because the bedclothes were being collected and changed. There was nothing immediately grim about the rooms, save that everyone had a roommate. My father would hate that—and with a single bathroom serving two rooms, he'd be sharing a bath with three other people.

I asked Katie how roommates, once overtaken by Alzheimer's, felt about living so close to someone else.

"It's rarely a problem," she said. "They don't really seem to notice."

I wondered how far gone my father would have to be not to notice something like that. Yet from the faces we'd seen so far, I believed her.

Most of the patients were gathered in the Bayview dining room, which looked out over the parking lot. (It's a widely followed rule: if a development is named Quail Run there will be no quail, and if a wing is named Bayview there will be no bay.) The dining room downstairs, though low-ceilinged, might have been part of a decent hotel, but this dining room looked more like a school cafeteria: tile floor, blank walls, some utilitarian tables and chairs. A burly attendant stood unmoving between two of the patients, as if posted there to keep them out of trouble, and a nurse or aide moved steadily among the others, answering requests. All the residents were old, a few were in wheelchairs, almost no one spoke. There were about twenty of them. A few glanced at a newspaper or magazine—though I guessed that, like my father, they weren't actually reading. Others stared at me and Katie, or out the window, or at nothing at all, and almost everyone's face looked blank and depressed. I found it devastating.

In spite of what I'd seen, before I left I asked Katie about the possibility of leaving my father there for a week or so, in case I had to go back to Ohio to take care of business.

"It's done all the time," she said. "We have an excellent respite care program."

But even as she answered, I knew it was impossible. I wasn't going to leave my father in a nursing home and assure him I'd be back in a week. Having lost track of what a week is, he'd think he'd been left for good. Besides, Katie confirmed what I'd already read, that people often plummet when first moved into a home. I wasn't so desperate that I was going to leave Dad in a place like that, even for a day. If I dropped him off he'd be one of the better-functioning clients in the Bayview wing—but how long would it take before he looked like everyone else?

I flossed some of my dad's teeth last night, after he got a bit of food stuck between them. Horrible stained old teeth, but still they gripped the floss. I kept at the job for over a minute before I found the irritant. All the while I was trying to get used to sticking my fingers in my father's mouth—and he must have felt awkward about it himself. Day by day I move closer to his decrepit old body.

Most of my father's money is wrapped up in his house, which he has now agreed to sell to Alan and Ellen. They've already taken out a mortgage and set up a closing date for later this month, but Dad, after many explanations, remains confused and worried about the transaction. He's seen what happened to Oliver after he signed over his rights, and wants a guarantee that he can remain at home. I describe the life tenancy Al has written into the contract, but Dad is still apprehensive.

When I take him over to sign the sales agreement, the lawyer asks him, "Are you doing this of your own free will, Joe? No one's making you do this, are they?"

Dad turns to me and says with a trace of both confusion and humor, "I don't know. Are you making me do this?"

"Not me," I say.

But in a way, I am. Both Al and I have prepped him for this signing, and we've hurried it along, fearing that dementia could undermine his legal right to make such a sale. I've reassured him many times that he can rely on Al and Joe Jr. and me to look after him—but in fact no legal document can guarantee that he'll be able to stay in his house as long as he wants. If we decide he has to go to a nursing home, off he goes. Neither a lease nor ownership can determine that. It depends on how long I can stick it out.

He signs, and I'm relieved when it's done. The house will remain in the family, and there will be money to pay for his care.

Dad gets up, I warm the bathroom, he showers and shaves. Through the half-open door I check to make sure he's putting on fresh underwear rather than slipping back into his wet incontinence underpants from last night. He dresses, he takes his medications, and soon after that he's on the couch, dozing off for most of the day. In many ways it's an infant's life, full of staring and sleeping.

The phone rings and I pick it up.

"Are you going crazy yet?"

"Lois Gilbert!"

"Well, you still sound cheerful. How's the drive to Australia going?"

Lois wants to know if I've had any days off, and I tell her that most weekdays I get out of the house and go to the library to write. "That's what I really need," I tell her, "a couple of hours a day over there to work on the novel."

Lois is a writer herself, with three published novels and another in the works, and she knows how much time I can spend "polishing that gravel," code for rewriting flawed material. "Are you getting anywhere?" she asks.

"I've worked on a couple of chapters. But I can't seem to take the characters back to my dad's house and let them percolate. It's like they're off on a cruise or something."

"Let 'em go. You should write something about your father."

By now I'm pacing around upstairs, using my headset. This is where I come when I want to talk in private. I tell Lois I've been keeping a journal, and she urges me to set everything down, record what my father says and everything he does. She asks if he gets under my skin.

"He's a great guy," I tell her. "But yes, sometimes."

She laughs. "You and your dad are the perfect pair of martyrs."

"Weren't you glad you looked after your father?"

"Sure, but I only did it for three weeks. You might be at this for years."

This hits me like a plank. *For years.*

In one breath she tells me I'm doing the right thing and my father is lucky to have me—and in the next that I'm nuts and I'll wear myself out. She's never been hobbled by consistency. "Are you meeting any women?" she asks.

"I don't meet anybody. And what would I do if I met someone?"

"Invite her over. You might look very attractive to a woman, taking care of your father like that."

"And then we could sneak into the kitchen and have a cup of tea."

"You could sneak upstairs. Anything could happen. There must be women at that library."

Though Lois never quite believes me, I've told her that after my last two painful breakups I feel removed from mating and breeding. All I want to do now is write every day and play some tennis. I'm going to join a club, I tell her.

"Is your father paying?"

"Absolutely."

"Excellent. You just keep listening to me."

Soon after my conversation with Lois I give up on the novel. It's dead, I can't deal with it. I have to believe in a story to write it, and I've lost touch with that book. Better, as Lois suggests, to record the turmoil that's right in front of me, the collapse of my father's mind.

A few days ago I went to visit the dementia unit in a second nursing home. I thought Fran, the woman who ran the place, was great—but for me there was no escaping the inert bodies and unresponsive faces of most of the residents. A walk through those corridors, or even through my father's living room, raises the inevitable question: What's the point of such a life?

I imagine that to a Christian or Muslim believer the point must be the afterlife that follows. Such faith would be a consolation, but I've never had any. To me it's this life or nothing. And as bad as it gets, I'll probably cling to it when I'm in Dad's condition or worse. Just like my father, I'll want to live, and I won't be thinking about the point of it.

When my son was growing up I read to him almost every night. We lay down together with the weight of his head against my chest, his hair damp and his attention sharp. If I started at the wrong place, Janir leapt on my mistake: *You read that already.* If I read by rote, thinking about something else, he knew and pulled me back: *Dad, read the story.* Year after year we continued. I was still reading to him at thirteen, at fourteen. At fifteen I lay on his bed beside him and read my own book while he read his. At sixteen we read in our own rooms, not far apart. When the first of us turned out his light and sang out "Hug in bed!" the other had to get up and give the hug.

When he was ten, after years of Tolkien and the Narnia tales, all of which had intrigued him and bored me, I picked up a book I'd loved as a teenager, C. S. Forester's *Lieutenant Hornblower*. It was an immediate success, the first book to please us equally—and now I've found a copy on my dad's bookshelves. It's a mass market paperback with tiny print and the pages turning brown, but I have such a history with the book I love just holding it. I show Dad the cover, with lanky young Hornblower in his tricorne hat, standing in the waist of the *Renown*. "Oh yes," my father says, "a very good book."

We don't lie down on his bed with it, but sit across from each other in the living room, each in a pool of light. We like the book from the first paragraph, in which Horatio Hornblower wears a uniform that looked "like it had been put on in the dark and not readjusted since." The crazy captain shows up on page two, and the plot immediately unfolds.

Through much of the day I don't know what to do with my father. He's rarely able to keep up a conversation anymore, and often just sits and stares. This is so unlike him it unnerves me. Sometimes I make forays into topics I think might interest him—history or economics or language—but I have to keep most of it aloft myself. Reading to him works out better. For thirty minutes at a time we are plunged into Forester's timeless world and seem to enjoy it equally. Of course I could be wrong about that. There is so much I can only guess at.

Later I think back on my own childhood. Did my father ever read to me in bed? Perhaps in the living room, before I went upstairs—but I can't remember that. He didn't get into bed with me or lie around with me or hold me. Didn't he want to?

In a folder full of old photos I find one of my mother, about fifteen, standing with a boyfriend in the backyard of her house on High Street in Columbus, Ohio, wearing a sleeveless cotton dress. Virginia, with a slender neck and one long bare arm, looks straight at the camera. She has circled the boy's high waist with her other arm, but leans slightly away from him. The boy, with his dorky haircut and glasses, radiates innocence. My mother radiates sex—and I know that within a year or two she'll be sleeping with someone much older. She had boyfriends, then lovers, and at nineteen married her first husband.

Virginia Thorndike with an early boyfriend, about 1930

My father, in contrast, seems to have emerged from a sexual and romantic void. I've never heard him mention a girlfriend from high school or college, or even from his first years in New York. I have a gossipy nature, a novelist's interest in the affairs of the heart—but it's hard for me to imagine Dad sitting on a porch swing with some girl, or in the backseat of his family's Model A. I'd like to hear reports like that about him, but there are none. He has never told them, and there are no photos of him with his arm around a girlfriend—or around my mother. Still, I'm on the lookout, and his files are thick. I've just started going through them.

Al comes down for three days, and his arrival lifts a weight from my chest. In the last few weeks I've noticed how eagerly I look forward to his e-mails. It's almost like getting mail from a lover. His is the name I look for in my Inbox, and when I see it I'm happy. I have backup, I have support, we're in this together. I can complain to Al at any time and send him accounts of Dad's mad behavior.

After our first dinner together Al washes the dishes, then sits down with his computer to work on an array of legal and financial documents. At one point he takes a break, gets out an oversized yellow pad, and writes out one of his Action Punch Lists, itemizing improvements to be made to the house. Al is organized to the core.

The three of us are sitting around after dinner when Joe Boyd calls. After a brief hello I pass the headset to my dad, who's sitting in the Monstrosity with his feet raised. The telephone rucks up his hair and confuses him, but he's clearly pleased to hear from his oldest friend.

Joe Boyd and Joe Thorndike. They met at the *Harvard Crimson* and have known each other for more than seventy years. For much of that time Joe Boyd has devoted himself to setting up a kind of alternate currency—the Boyd System—and my father has consulted with him about it and edited some of his writing. I wonder how long it will take Joe to figure out that my father's memory is going.

Quite a while, apparently, because after ten minutes he's still doing all the talking. My dad responds with an occasional *Yes* and *Sure,* and eventually he asks me to write down a couple of numbers. I pick up the other phone and write them down as reported: they're the numbers of two bills before Congress relating to some trade policy, and Joe has plenty to say about them. He talks and talks. After a while I hang up my phone, and Dad goes on repeating his monosyllables. He laughs a couple of times as well, but I don't think Joe ever asks him anything that would require a real answer. Dad can still come out with "Yes, yes, that's what we want," and "We're getting it all down," but his eyes are closed and his face tight. He gives a little moan, but the call continues.

"Well," he says, "thank you."

And, "Yes, we've got it all down."

And, "You what?"

And, "Oh, okay."

Then a long silence in which Dad says nothing at all for three or four minutes. I glance at Al, who mouths back, *Is he asleep?* I can't tell. Dad's head is twisted so far to one side he looks like he's been shot. Finally I get up to check the other phone—and Joe Boyd is still talking! Dad slumps forward, then arches his back and sits upright again.

"Okay," he murmurs.

Still it continues, for another five minutes. By now Dad's expression is softening, and he no longer moves at all. He's asleep, and when I pick up the other phone, there's only a dial tone.

After Al leaves I'm blue. He won't be back until April, and I'm alone with my silent father.

I've always claimed a happy childhood, at least through the age of ten or eleven. I did well in school, I had friends, my family was stable. Then something went awry. It was touch, I think: not enough of it. The early photos show that I was held as a young boy, but later I stand aside, a little like my grandfather. Where did this come from?

When I was seven or eight I was still getting buzzed every night. This was a game in which my father carried me around the living room with my arms outstretched like an airplane, as I strafed anything live in the room: my mother, my brother, Nana, Bourbon the dog and Panther the cat. If Dad was playful enough we swept past my mother's bronze bust on the desk, past the origami mobile, past the flowers on the mantelpiece as I made my best dive-bomber noises. Al, of course, had an equal turn.

I've long assumed it was my father who pulled back from this physical contact, but in one of his old notebooks I find this line from the year I was ten: "Alan still loves to be buzzed, but John is not as interested as before." Could I have already entered my decade of physical isolation? Could I have chosen this myself?

Dad stopped buzzing me and never took me in his arms again. My mother would come up to say good night, but I don't remember either of my parents climbing into bed with me. Maybe when I was younger, because I'm sure they read me stories. I also had Nana, and my brother to wrestle, and our big beautiful Irish setter. All that sustained me until I left Saugatuck Elementary and was sheep-dipped into Bedford Junior High with its hoods and bullies. I was a small kid and didn't do well there or on the bus, where I was teased hard.

I needed someone to talk to, and I needed to be held. At least that's what I think now. I was headed for a teenage desert in which I never touched anyone. Sex was coming into my body and mind, but that only made me shyer. Off I went to boarding school, and almost four years would pass before I kissed a girl, or put a hand on one, or felt her hand on me.

The school was Deerfield Academy in western Massachusetts. I honor Deerfield for how it allowed me, a tiny kid, to play competitive sports on lower-level teams. The fall of my freshman year there were nine soccer teams—Varsity, JV, JV Reserve, Leagues, Seniors, Juniors A, B, C and D—and I played on Junior D. But like every other team we had both practice and game uniforms, a full schedule of home and away games, and a coach who reported at the nightly meeting on how we'd fared. All that was great for someone who loved to play sports but was not very skilled.

All the same, I was hazed and humiliated at Deerfield during my first two years, forced into "mouse fights" by classmates as large as grown men. In those fights, some other small kid and I would be goaded—our ears tweaked, our scalps nuggied, our arms twisted hard—until we exploded into a pair of desperate headlocks, each trying to squeeze the other into submission, trying not to be the worst weenie in the school.

Apart from those fights, or when banging up against kids on the soccer field, we lived in a world of unspoken but strict prohibitions against contact. You didn't touch another guy: not his arm, not his shoulder, God forbid not the back of his neck. Not his *foot*. I watch high school kids today and they're wonderfully relaxed. It's not just the girls who throw their arms around each other, guys do it too. They might make a joke of it, but they're touching, they're giving their bodies some play. I had a good friend at Deerfield, a classmate I actually talked to about girls, about our families, about how we *felt*. I believe this was remarkable for the time. But we never hung onto each other or touched in any way. At the end of the school year, and the start of the next, we shook hands.

What were my parents thinking, to send me to a school where every sensuous response to life was pounded out of me? I understand that not everything was the school's fault, or my parents'. In part it was the age—and ten years later the sixties would sweep in and rescue my ass with its exuberance, its sex, its endorsement of the body. But I was only thirteen when my parents sent me off to an alien world.

Years ago I asked my father, "Whose idea was it for me to go away to school, yours or mine?"

"Actually, it was your mother's idea."

That knocked me flat. It was my *mother*. And the reason, I think now, is that she was looking ahead to her freedom. If I went away to boarding school, so would my brother, and we'd both be out of the house four years earlier. For a time after I heard that, I wanted to throttle her. At least my father believed in such places. He thought I'd do well at Deerfield, and of course he never heard about my humiliations in Chapin Hall at the hands of Dary Dunham and Mac Walker—because I never told him. I never told any adult. *No squealing* is the first rule of the weak, disguised as a kind of honor.

When I went home on vacations my parents should have seen that something was wrong. *I* can see it instantly, in a series of photos I find in one of my dad's file cabinets. I'm sitting on the couch with my arms folded, sullen in my crewneck sweater. I'm almost grown, and resist my mother as she leans toward me, clearly reaching out in some way. I'm not going to let her in. It's too late for that, because by now I've ingrained a culture whose backbone is self-reliance and detachment. I've made a little soldier of myself, armored top to bottom.

Home for Christmas from boarding school, 1959

This, at least, is what I see in these photos as an adult. At seventeen, I probably had no idea what was going on.

I still blame my mother for being selfish—but as a parent I understand something of the battle she fought, having struggled to balance my own need for freedom with my son's need for attention. There were times I didn't give him enough, or not all he wanted: times when I was too wrapped up in some romance or project. I think for most parents the conflict is unavoidable, because if all you do is devote yourself to your kids, you won't have a life they can emulate. Children need attention, but they also need to see parents who are making their way through the world. It's an uncrackable nut, and I give my mother some leeway because of it. I felt deceived when I learned it had been her idea to ship me off—but by then I understood how like her I was, how the demands of parenthood could wear at me. Still, I never thought of sending Janir away to school. We were having way too much fun for that.

My mother must have been busy through my youth, but I don't remember her that way. She was calm and relaxed, and apparently sailed through college, graduating Phi Beta Kappa from Barnard when I was eleven, then moving on to med school at NYU. Medical textbooks lined her bookshelves at home, but I have no memories of her holing up with them over long weekends, or even reading them in the living room at night. Maybe after I went to bed.

In all her years of internship, residency and practice, she never took me to visit any of the hospitals where she spent so much time. She did tell an occasional galvanizing story about life in the operating room: the time a surgeon "put his thumb through the patient's heart," covering doctors and nurses with a spray of pulsing blood until the tear was sewn up. And there was the night she came home looking weary and confessed to us after dinner, "I lost a patient today." Perhaps the surgeon had done something wrong, or she had, or maybe it was only bad luck, but an old woman had died on the table when she might not have, and my mother took it hard.

As an anesthesiologist she worked every day with lungs, and I can still remember the bright color photos in a magazine she once brought home, of the dissected lungs of smokers and nonsmokers, the latter pink and the former a hard-to-believe charcoal color. It was a straightforward ploy to stop me from smoking, and it worked. To this day I sometimes cringe at the image that jumps to mind, when I'm standing close to an inhaling smoker, of the black inside of their lungs.

My mother went off to work every day the way fathers did on television. She disappeared, usually before anyone else in the house got up, and reappeared in the evening. Both my parents had jobs. I saw them come and go and didn't worry about it. I was that kid on a bike, that kid in a rowboat, wrapped up in my own adventures. But I did like telling people, "My mother is a doctor." To this day I like to explain that my mother worked, that she went back to school when I was eight, that she was an anesthesiologist.

Dad never throws anything out, but behind his back I've started tossing some of the clutter that fills his house: cracked old plates and plastic cups, an old hand plane hopelessly rusted, wood putty hard as marble, a dozen scabrous toothbrushes, a hundred ballpoint pens that don't work, a pack of cards with a note under a rubber band saying *5o,* a tide table from 1989, a box of ancient keys carefully labeled *Unknown.* An old briefcase without a handle or clasp, two dozen light cotton plaid shirts all worn through at the collar, six torn lampshades and catalogs to sink a dinghy. A telephone answering machine that's been replaced, and the manual for that machine, and the manuals for the two previous machines. Two old editing machines for 8 mm film, and a projector I struggled with for an hour. I briefly got it running, and was rewarded with the velvety slow-motion dives of my mother into a blue Vero Beach swimming pool in 1954, pikes and layouts from the one- and three-meter boards. My mother was the 1932 junior diving champion of Ohio. Unfortunately, the projector broke down halfway through the first reel, and the many other reels, though carefully saved by my father, remain inaccessible.

Sundowning is the depressed state that often overwhelms the memory-impaired around dusk, and most days my father sinks into it around four or five in the afternoon. He lies on his bed with a vacant stare, unhappy and distant, never a glance my way. This afternoon, when I suggested we go down to Red River Beach, he said "Not now," even his politeness drained out of him.

But I didn't give up. I came back a second and third time, urging him, telling him he'd like it—and finally he agreed to go.

Just getting out of the house into the open air made a difference, and by the time we parked in front of the beach, with its gulls and ducks and piles of empty whelk shells, he was in much better spirits. Helping things out, the gray sky lifted in the west, and toward Monomoy the waters turned aquamarine, looking more like the Caribbean than Cape Cod in February. We sat in the car with the heater running, and talk came easy. I've been reading more about World War II, and asked Dad again about his work as a *Life* correspondent. He told me about some nights he slept in a foxhole on the beach at Anzio, under shells that blew past like freight trains. I'd never heard this from him before, and wondered if he was mixing up several stories. I didn't care. I was glad to see him in a livelier mood, and glad I'd pressured him to come.

Gerry Elovitz, back when we talked after his second interview with Dad, had no doubts about what my father needed. He needed socialization on a regular basis, and Gerry urged me to take him to the Community Center whether he wanted to go or not. "Once he starts going, he'll like it."

I argued against this. I explained that my father didn't want to play cards or bingo, or talk to other seniors. Whether that would be good for him or not, he wasn't interested.

"Don't ask him," Dr. Elovitz insisted. "Just take him over there."

I'm sure he didn't just toss off that advice. He's dealt with thousands of people with dementia, and believed I should twist my father's arm because I knew what was best for him. In fact, that's exactly how it worked out today when I took him to the beach. I prevailed upon Dad to leave the house, and now I'm glad I did.

When I was a child my father almost never pressured me to do anything, and the dedication of my second novel reads, "For JJT, who always let us choose." So now, when I can either coax my father or let him be, I'm slow to tell him what he should do with his life. It's true that his mind is going, but who's to say how he should spend his days? Who's to say he shouldn't sit in a chair and do nothing? Who's to say, even, that he ought to do things that will make him happy?

Coercion is the topic that fascinates me, the one I never resolve. Sometimes I consult with Sandy Weymouth about it— even if I already know what he's going to say.

"Weymouth, what am I going to do? My father's falling apart. Here's a guy who's never been bored in his life, and all he wants to do is sit in his chair. Is this what your father does?"

"Sure. Hours a day."

"Do you worry about it?"

"Not really. It's his life, and I try to give him exactly what he wants. But I don't do it until he asks for it."

"But *your* dad can ask, his mind isn't going."

"Are you telling me your father doesn't know what he wants?"

"He knows," I say. "He wants to be left alone."

"Okay, leave him alone. What could be simpler?"

"It's never simple. Because sometimes I can persuade him to do things that make him feel better." I tell Sandy the story of our trip to Red River Beach.

"If it were me I'd leave him alone. I wouldn't give him any food, I wouldn't give him any water, I wouldn't dress him, I wouldn't do *anything* until he asked. Then, I'd do everything."

"He never asks for food and never asks for water."

"How long have you waited?"

"Not very long. Sometimes he asks for a cup of black coffee."

"Do you give it to him?"

"Decaf," I admit. "Which isn't what he wants, but he's not supposed to have caffeine."

"Says who?"

"The doctors. The pamphlets, the Internet."

"Your father asks for a goddamn cup of coffee, *give it to him.* What are you protecting him from?"

"What about his medications?" I'm pacing around on the snow-covered lawn outside, my headset on under a wool hat, my boots crunching loudly. "You're not suggesting I wait until he asks for those?"

"Does he want to take them?"

"I put them in front of him with a glass of water, and he takes them. Before his memory went he took them on his own. He tried not to miss a dose."

"That's persuasive," Sandy says. "But he hasn't forgotten the ocean. If he wants to go there he could tell you."

"I don't think he would."

"Why not give it a try? Give it a week and see what he asks for. Let him get hungry, I bet he's going to ask for food. Keep giving him his medications, but stop forcing everything else on him. We do this to old people the same way we do it to kids. Quit making him do what you want him to do, and let him decide."

"You make it sound easy, Weymouth. But it wouldn't be that easy. He'd sit around and be miserable, and then I'd be miserable. And after a couple of days of that—I'd think you're an asshole."

Sandy laughs. "That's fair. I'll live with that."

I love Weymouth for the vehemence of his convictions, and I'm half persuaded by what he says. I'll probably give his ideas a try—but I doubt if it'll be long before I go back to putting the subtle thumbscrews to Dad to try to liven him up. Who wants a spaced-out, disconsolate parent?

Out of the blue Dad calls me over to the couch to explain how he has always bought gas at the Chatham Mobil station, how he has them fill his tank when he goes, how he often steps inside and talks to the girl there. "I think it's good," he says, "because I've been going there so long. All these years, I always go there. I talk to them, so I have a relationship there and that helps."

I'm just noting how coherent he sounds, and how he has used that up-to-date word *relationship,* when he comes to his point: "I think it helps with my throat. With my coughing."

Increasingly he gets his body mixed up with the rest of the world. This morning, because I'm going to the library and he'll be here alone, I go over the use of the new walkie-talkies. Talking back and forth has proved too complex for him, but each unit has a call button that sets off a ring at the other end, and since the library is only three hundred yards away, I could make it back in five minutes. We practiced this a couple of days ago, and now I set his unit on the table in front of him.

"So Dad, let's try this again. Let's say you need me and Harriet isn't here. No one is here, and you want me to come back from the library. What do you do?"

For a moment he looks puzzled. It's another test, and he has failed so many. Eventually he lifts his forefinger—and touches it to a spot under his nose. He's tentative about it, but that's his answer: "I have to press here."

I come close to laughing, but hold back. His look is so hopeful, like a child taking a wild guess. And when I put the walkie-talkie in his hands he immediately finds the right button.

At bedtime we go over his usual concerns. What's *that?* he wants to know. Just the VCR, I assure him. He peers vaguely at the bookshelf that covers the entire wall at the far end of the room. "Isn't there something we have to do about . . . *that?*"

I pick out some books, inspect them and set them back in place. There's not much I can say when he starts worrying. Finally he settles back against his pillow, and I stand beside him with my hand on his shoulder. I say what I say every night, "I'll see you in the morga-dorga"—lingo from the years my son was in junior high—and go out into the living room. But only a minute later he calls me back. There's something else he wants to ask.

"Isn't someone else here? Isn't someone waiting in the kitchen?"

"I don't think so, Dad."

"Yes," he says, "it's Mitt Romney. I think he's here. He's very helpful."

Mitt is the dapper governor of Massachusetts. My dad is serious, but I have some fun with it and say, "I imagine he's pretty busy these days. Not much time for house calls."

"Are you sure?"

"Pretty sure. And the guy *is* a Republican."

"Yes, I know, but he's good. I think he's here."

"I could look, but I really don't think so."

"I thought we might have him in the refrigerator."

At this I burst out laughing. "Dad, what can I say? Definitely not in the refrigerator."

He thinks it over. He looks puzzled and unsure. As the animation fades from his face he takes his cover and twitches it up to his chin with his delicate hands. "Somewhere out there," he says, without the least hint of reprimand.

Talking to the woman who runs the local Alzheimer's Services, one sentence from her brings me up sharp: *It's just beginning for you.*

Dad wants to go outdoors. He can't quite put it in words, but there's something he wants to look at, something having to do with a corner of his property that the town officials have neglected in some way. So I get him dressed and we head outside, Dad behind his walker. Once off the ramp he heads straight for his car, so apparently we're headed somewhere. I help him get in, put the walker in the backseat, sit down behind the wheel, and ask him where we're going.

"Are we going somewhere?"

"You decide, Dad. I'll take you wherever you want."

He looks right and left. "Go left," he says at the street, and from that point on I let him decide everything. Seeing the sign for the Cranberry Valley Golf Course, he has me turn in. He wants to see if they've put up the plaque to commemorate my brother's celebrated hole-in-one last summer, but the fairways are covered with snow and there's no one at the clubhouse. When we return to the road he says "Turn right." Then, a quarter mile later, "I want to go to Orleans."

Okay, a verbalized plan. I like this. We take the Mid-Cape highway, get off at Orleans, and from there he decides every turn. "Right here," he says, then, "Left here," and we're headed for Nauset Heights and the McGees' house, where we've gone to the beach so many times. The lane to the head of the stairs is empty, so I drive down it and park as close as I can get. It's a dicey walk, fifteen feet over snow and ice, but our reward is a sturdy railing, a wide blue sea below and the full bath of Cape light, almost as soft in midwinter as it is in August. My dad's gaze drifts out over the open water. Here a man can stand, as Thoreau wrote, "and put all America behind him."

This is the beach where we've agreed that my father's ashes will be thrown—but we say nothing about that.

Later, driving home, I wonder what it would be like, in my advanced old age, to live with Janir and his wife, LL. How far would I let it go? Would I decide at some point that the time had come to swallow some tequila and forty of those Nembutals, still saved in Dad's cloth bag? I think again about returning the pills to his closet, but I still don't want to. If he asked, I'd do it in a minute, but the topic seems forgotten. Now I'm driving along with my dad beside me, all choked up about what I would say to Janir on my own deathbed: how much I love him, how I adored him when he was a boy and we spent our life together.

Janir is going to be a great father. Just six months ago I could have cared less about being a grandfather, but I have an inkling now of how much I might like it—and how beautiful it will be to see Janir in love with his own child. What better way for him to understand how much I loved *him?*

According to the literature my father suffers from aphasia, agnosia, anosognosia and dressing apraxia. Aphasia is language impairment, agnosia the failure to understand the source or meaning of pain, anosognosia the loss of self-awareness, and dressing apraxia the inability to dress himself according to the usual norms, with shirt beneath sweater, underwear beneath pants, and so on.

A dinner of scrod, red peppers, new potatoes and steamed fresh spinach, everything on the table in twenty-five minutes. "I'll never eat all that," Dad said, as he often does. He ate every ounce of it, with some carrot cake for dessert. But the thrill of the meal was his bright look. He'd been lying in his bedroom most of the day, nearly inert, and I expected one of those meals in which he doesn't say twenty words. Now he chatted about the food, looked like his old self, and after eating had a story to tell me.

It was about a trip he'd taken years ago from Iceland to Greenland. He was rowing in a boat, he said, and picking things up at stops along the way. "Things from other people who were coming down from the north with their contributions. Things they'd gotten from other people coming down from even farther north, with *their* contributions. It took a long time, going along and stopping and picking up all these things. It was a long trip. But we went along and came to the St. Lawrence River, and people were coming down from the north, you see, with their contributions. Then the St. Croix River, and they were making stops, and picking things up. The St. Lawrence River, and the St. Croix River, I think it was the St. Croix, and people were bringing things down from even farther north."

I loved this story. "What were those contributions?" I asked.

"Foodstuffs. We were picking them up."

"Was this before I was born?"

"Yes, before you were born. Long before. From there . . . where was it? Some body of water. I think it was the Mississippi. We went down the Mississippi and went to—some place. To a town. There was a town. Some town."

He paused. The story was coming more slowly. Then he got it: "Hannibal. We went to Hannibal. We were there a long time because there were so many contributions. We had a boat, or . . . we had a. . . ."

"A raft?"

"That's right, that was it, we had a raft. People kept coming in, coming in from the north, you see."

I could listen to him tell stories like this all night. I don't care how batty he sounds, I just hope for some engagement and a vivid look on his face. It can still break my heart to see his mind, that formidable instrument, fly around like a chickadee in a windstorm—but the real disasters are depression and grief. For this night, at least, he was happy.

Only a night later we had another sprightly conversation. It started when I quoted Ovid on the cruel nature of romance—"She who flies from me I follow, and she who follows me I fly from"—and I mispronounced the poet's name.

"I think that's Ah-vid, not Oh-vid," my father said, and the dictionary proved him right. Oh well, I've been saying it wrong for forty years. I love it that my dad still corrects me, and also that he knew that the emperor during Ovid's time was Augustus, and that Ovid was eventually banished by him to an outpost of the empire, a place where they spoke no Latin. Dad, though confused about so many things, has a pretty good grip on the Romans. He claims that the U.S. has entered the late stage of empire, analogous to the fall of Rome. What signaled the end for the Romans, he told me last week, was when the baths at Caracalla ran out of hot water. We joke about this sometimes when he gets ready for his morning shower.

And this same erudite and charming guy, an hour after dinner, asks me as he sits on his bed, "What is it I'm supposed to do now?"

March

Sometimes I wonder what it would be like if I were looking instead after my elderly mother, if she'd been the one to survive and come down with Alzheimer's. I'm sure we'd have talked with far more intimacy than I can wrest from my father—but I can also imagine how needy and difficult she might have turned. She never had my father's restraint and equanimity. Of course, there's no knowing when Dad might go awry himself. No matter his natural reserve, no matter how gentle and decent he has always shown himself, such character traits are no match for this disease, or so I've read. Once the brain is colonized by Alzheimer's, all moderation can fly out the window, and the mildest-mannered patient become hopelessly irascible.

I register this, yet hold onto the belief that my father will be different, that his lifelong nature will prevail. It has so far. Occasionally he panics a little, but I see no sign of bitterness or anger. It seems to me the disease would have to reach his very brainstem before it could wipe out his essential decency.

Young Joe, as my father calls him, has arrived for a visit. Like Dad, he's a historian. He's been finishing his dissertation on FDR's tax policies, and is about to earn his PhD. Dad hoped he would bring his two-year-old daughter Eliza, but the trip was too long and the girl too wild, so Joe has come alone. Dad's happy to see him, but also confused. I think he's reminded of our August reunions, because now he's convinced that the rest of the family will soon arrive.

Joe, the only cook among the brothers, prepares a cioppino filled with clams, shrimp, scallops and cod. Dad shines at the dinner table, and after the meal he remains alert. He talks about his parents and about working for Henry Luce at *Time*. He makes suggestions about an article Joe wants to write, and tells of a novel he wants to write himself, about two men fighting for control of an uninhabited island in the Pacific. Tonight he still has ambitions.

I've told Joe many stories of Dad's confusion, and he's seen the signs himself. But now our father is talking like a professor about the policies of Wilson, Hoover and Roosevelt. It's Joe who brings this out, I'm sure. They are the intellectuals of the family, as was Joe's mother. I was twenty-three when Joe was born, so we spent little time together when he was young. More in recent years, though, and not long ago we shared a pair of odd confessions. Joe told me that he's always felt that Al and I have been closer to Dad than he has, and I said that I've long thought of him as my father's truest offspring, the one who can get Dad to talk. Of course, our father would never show or confess to the least favoritism toward any of us—but it's Joe who has him talking tonight. I'm happy about this, glad to see him come out of his shell.

The next morning he's agitated. He wants to go outside, no matter that rain is sweeping across the driveway. He parks his walker in front of the door, stares out at the drowned morning, then announces to me and Joe that he wants to look around in the sunroom, an enclosed but unheated space. His two over-sized file cabinets are out there, and I clear away some of my tools so he can reach them. He's wearing his coat and hat, I plug in an electric heater, and the cold doesn't seem to bother him. Indeed, he barely notices me. He's standing in front of the far cabinet, lifting out pieces of paper, fingering them and putting them back. Later he pulls a chair over, sits down on it and begins to explore one of the lower drawers.

As I watch from the kitchen, my tenderness for him grows. He pulls out one sheet of paper after another, inspects them in the solemn way of a young child who has not yet learned to read, and returns them to their folders. He spends almost an hour at this, and eventually asks me to bring all the papers from that drawer into the living room. I transfer them into a cardboard box, set the box on the coffee table, and that evening, as Joe cooks dinner, I start to look through the papers myself.

The very first sheet, lying on top, is a 1948 memo to my father from Henry Luce, with his comments on an article Malcolm Cowley was writing about Ernest Hemingway. In the forties my father worked with many well-known writers of the time, including John Kenneth Galbraith, John Dos Passos, Whittaker Chambers, James Thurber and Winston Churchill.

He worked with all the early photographers at *Life* as well: Peter Stackpole, Margaret Bourke-White, Dmitri Kessel, George Silk, Nina Leen, Henri Cartier-Bresson, Alfred Eisenstaedt, Milton Greene, Philippe Halsman, Robert Capa, Gjon Mili, Carl Mydans and many others.

I've been aware since I was a teenager of his connections to famous people—though by the late fifties, at *American Heritage* and *Horizon*, he was working with writers better known in academic or artistic circles: the historians Bruce Catton, J. H. Plumb and H. R. Trevor-Roper, along with Irving Stone, William Harlan Hale, Walter Kerr and Ben Shahn.

Although I know their names, Dad has never told me stories about any of them. He doesn't gossip and never says anything about what interests me most, the people he worked with. I know that when Churchill came out with *The Gathering Storm*, the first of his volumes about the war, Dad helped him distill the book into six long excerpts, which were published in *Life* in successive issues in the spring of 1948. But now, when I ask him for stories about Winston, there's not much he can tell me.

Joe Thorndike at his desk at Life, *July 11, 1947.* Photo by Bill Sumits, courtesy of *Life* Photo Archive, Time Inc.

"Did he come to your office," I ask, "or did you go to where he was staying?"

A pause. "I think he must have come to the office."

"And was he helpful?"

"Quite helpful. He was—quite helpful. He did like to drink."

"You mean he was drunk?"

"No, I wouldn't say that."

His answers are rarely specific, perhaps because he can't remember. I've waited too long to ask my questions, and now no one from those years is still alive. Every one of the writers and photographers named above is dead. Henry Luce is dead, and his wife Clare Booth Luce, and the two managing editors at *Life* who preceded my father, John Shaw Billings and Dan Longwell. Dad, I believe, is the last survivor from the magazine's early years.

Why, I ask myself now, didn't I come and spend a month with my father when he could still hold a conversation? Even a year ago I could have learned plenty if I'd asked him more questions. Instead I trundled along, too busy with my own life. I never went to visit him in Maine, or to Florida in the winter, and when I came to the Cape I threw myself into everything except these files. Dad would have shown them to me gladly, I think, but I never asked. We're all warned about this: Better ask the questions while you have the chance—and I didn't.

I think of my father when he was young, the beloved child of an older couple, a solitary boy with not enough friends. He rose through ambition and the power of his mind, and lived a broad intellectual life at the center of the publishing world—yet he was always devoted to his family. He could talk to Winston Churchill during the day, then come home on the 6:12 train with presents for his boys. On Saturday morning he'd crouch on the lawn and renew his ancient battle with the crabgrass, and watch over us as we swam.

Few old people remain connected to the channels of power and fame. I think of our most famous Alzheimer's patient, President

Reagan, in the final years of his life, getting up in the morning, eating breakfast, taking a walk around the grounds. It's what most of us come to in the end: we have our family and friends, we have our children, we cultivate our garden. I've always believed in simplicity, and still claim not to care about a dramatic, more exciting life—but consider my fascination with the people my father knew and worked with. Money, fame, power and involvement: I'd love to have more of it all.

I'm steadily surprised—as is my brother Joe—at how relaxed Dad is about being naked. He doesn't react at all when I come into the bathroom to check up on him. He'll sit on the toilet, pissing slowly, or stand like a jaybird in front of the shower, unaware of his body or unconcerned about it.

I asked the head of one of the dementia units I visited last month if this change in modesty was common. "Oh, sure," she said. "That all fades away. I could run a completely nude unit here and none of them would care."

My father, who seems so independent, has hardly spent a year alone since 1939. Soon after his painful divorce from my mother he courted and married Margery Darrell, an editor at *Horizon*. Joe Jr. was born in 1965 and grew up with Margery's two sons by an earlier marriage. After ten years Dad and Margery separated, and I thought he would retire from the world of romance. Instead he met Jane.

Jane had her demands, but they were easy for my father to meet. She liked attention. She liked to be looked after, and Dad was good at that. *Born to serve*, Al and I used to joke, after watching him take care of everyone he loved—including us.

In recent years, as Jane's health declined, my father spent more and more time with her. Though he didn't sell his house on the Cape and move in with her in Connecticut, as she wanted him to do, he stayed there for weeks at a time, running errands, cooking meals and answering her frequent calls. Her family had hired some women to help, but only my father would do. "I want Joe," she repeated, and though by then his own health was giving out, he did his best.

Given their long history I find it bizarre that Jane, who died with millions, didn't leave my father a dime. I asked Dad about it only once. "No sense worrying about that," he said, and the subject was closed.

And the fact is that for almost thirty years Jane paid my father in another coin. She was spoiled, but she was also lively and fun, exactly the blithe spirit my father loved to be around. She brought out a side of him my brothers and I rarely saw. Two Christmases ago in Vermont, Al paused outside his office door to listen in on Dad, who was talking to Jane on the phone. My father has a dry and subtle sense of humor, but the laughter coming out of Al's office was bubbly, at times almost a giggle. Dad doesn't like to stay on the phone, but he stayed on with Jane. "It was like listening in on a teenager," Al said—and by then Dad and Jane had been together for more than twenty-five years.

She loved a good prank. Back in the days when telegrams were delivered over the phone, she had me call her cousin and pretend to be a Western Union operator. We'd written out the message together in the archest telegram style, recounting the loss of the family silver, all gone, stolen in the night. The call raised a hell of a tempest.

Her lightheartedness, I think, was her response to some devastating blows, including the deaths of two of her brothers when she was young, and later of two nephews who committed suicide, four years apart to the day. And by far the worst, the nightmare of every parent, one of her daughters was killed in college, struck by a car at a dangerous crosswalk.

By the time she met my father, Jane didn't want to talk about any of that. God knows how much she had grieved. But the years had gone by, as they had for my father after his two troubled marriages, and now Jane wanted to laugh and have fun. She was a smoker and a drinker, and didn't want to talk about her calamities any more than Dad wanted to talk about his. They reached an understanding and made each other happy—which made the rest of us happy as well.

Finally a hint of spring. The ground is still covered with snow, but we've had our first day of forty degrees. As I opened the front door this morning I surprised a pair of mourning doves under the bird feeder. They exploded into the air and clattered away toward the trees, and just describing this to Dad brought a smile and an animated look to his face. It makes me long for the time when he can go outside and stay there comfortably, when he can watch the birds and the year's new growth.

I've been reading about Alzheimer's in David Shenk's portrait of the disease, *The Forgetting*. The usual progression has been charted quite precisely, and it starts in the hippocampus. This two-inch structure, nestled deep within the brain's temporal lobes, is what enables us to secure current thoughts and impressions as long-lasting memories. During brain development, it's the last component to gain protective myelin, and one of the last to work effectively—which is why few people can remember much from before the age of three. It's also the least myelinated part of the brain, and one of the first to have its myelin stripped. Thus, memory loss is almost always the first sign of encroaching Alzheimer's.

The next part of the brain to be affected is the nearby amygdala, seat of such primitive emotions as fear, anger and craving.

Slowly—it can take a decade, possibly longer—the temporal, parietal and frontal lobes will all be taken over by the gooey plaques and neurofibrillary tangles characteristic of the disease, and each step will erode some new social, mental or physical skill in the patient.

In a terrible reversal of the brain's development, an Alzheimer's patient unlearns everything he or she learned as a child, in almost exactly the reverse order. At one to three months a baby can hold up its head. At two to four months he can smile. At six to ten months she can sit without assistance, at a year walk without help, at two to three years control her bowels, at three to four years her bladder. The continuing progression is familiar to anyone who has raised a child: can use a toilet on his own, can adjust the temperature of bath water, can dress himself, and so on.

That's my dad right there: he can no longer put on his clothes by himself—or if I let him, he's likely to botch the job. Sometimes he can adjust the temperature of the bath water, and sometimes not. Ahead lies inescapable regression.

We often think of old age as a return to a kind of childhood, as a time we can relinquish many of our duties. As we grew up we learned to follow schedules and perform chores. We were told to keep our clothes on, to sit up straight, to say please, to tie our shoes and pick up our toys. We learned to make our beds, to mow the lawn, to take out the trash, to bring in the dog and put out the cat. We grew up bending to the yoke of adulthood.

But now that Dad has no dog or cat, now that I take out the trash and he's free to do whatever he likes, a nasty trick has been played on him. He can't relax. He's fretful and full of compulsions. The trouble is, he's still aware of what he's losing.

He's had a bad couple of days since Joe's departure. Joe explained that he'd come back soon and bring his daughter,

Eliza, but I don't think Dad is reassured by such plans. *Soon* for him is a black box, and what he sees now is that Joe is no longer here.

When I get come home from the library at four he's just getting into bed. I coax him into watching some *Victory at Sea* on tape, from the television show of the early fifties, but before the segment ends he's gone. Not just asleep, but fallen off the end of the earth. His face shows no sign of rest or dreams, only a flatness that looks like defeat. I fix an early dinner and soon have it on the table, but *"No,"* he says when I wake him. "No dinner for me tonight. None." He's so definitive about it I take his plate back to the kitchen, then sit down and eat my meal alone.

Night falls and wind rattles the windows. I worry about my father, but I also think about something Joe said when he was here, that Alzheimer's patients sometimes need to crash. They need to give up for a while, and stop rising to the occasion.

My questions about coercion remain, especially on the topic of food. Every day Harriet and I press my father to eat. What do you say to some soup for lunch? Here's a little snack. Would you like a banana? Time for another glass of water. How about some Ensure? We've got some great clam chowder. And after dinner the closer, the one that always works: How about some coffee almond fudge ice cream?

Sandy Weymouth has told me how his mother's attendants, and his own brothers, were always pumping food down his mother's throat. Not literally, but they urged her to eat whether she was hungry or not. She was ninety-four, then ninety-five years old, she was tired and infirm and didn't care about eating. But food was gospel and eating her duty. *Come on Mom, just one more bite.*

What if my father wants to crash for good? What if he's deeply tired of rising to the occasion, and his way out is to forget about food? I consider this, but I doubt it will be long before I slide another plate in front of him. It's the habit of care, and the assumption that everyone must eat. Though I question this, I'm tied to the wheel myself.

Dad is completely beat. He still takes a shower in the morning, still comes to the table for breakfast, but then he sits down in his chair, or more likely goes back to bed. He doesn't read anything, doesn't say anything, just lies there with his head back and his eyes closed. I go to the library for three hours, and Harriet is here for two of them. She's bright and enthusiastic and gets him to eat, stretch and talk a little. But by the time I get back his late-afternoon funk has swallowed him. He doesn't want to drive to the ocean: "Not right now," he says. He doesn't want to watch a video: "Not right now."

Some years ago a friend in Ohio died of colorectal cancer, a long and painful death. Step by step she withdrew into her ordeal, refusing all medication, even analgesics. Near the end she lay in bed, almost unreachable, beside a mutual friend, Kathy Galt. They'd known each other for years, their children were the same age, they had talked and talked—but now, as Kathy spoke, Elizabeth responded with a whisper. Kathy bent closer as faintly, with great difficulty, Elizabeth said, "Words . . . take away."

I've been trying to rouse my father, to entertain him, to entice him out of his blank state—yet perhaps it's no blank state at all, but a tremendous battle he has taken up in his own quiet way. Perhaps all the offers I make are mere interruptions to that battle. I'm always trying to maneuver him back into the world, but maybe all of it, even talking, takes something away.

After another feast last night, with Dad finishing every morsel of salmon and yams, he made his way to the bathroom, his farts sounding loose enough to be trouble. He closed the door behind him and for twenty minutes I heard nothing. When I asked how he was doing, he announced that he was fine, everything was fine. Another ten minutes brought the same answer. But when I finally opened the door I could see he was confused. He was gripping the handles of the toilet's safety frame, his pants lay on the floor and his Depends were nowhere in sight.

His underwear was in the toilet bowl, now weighing five pounds. Dad resisted having me clean his bottom, but I cleaned it anyway. This was not, I told him, nearly as messy as the time my mother came to visit me on my farm in Chile, caught a bug and suffered two straight days of delirium and diarrhea. Kind of a ghastly story, but the situation was faintly analogous, and I wanted to let him know I could take care of him, that it wasn't going to kill me to wipe his ass. I didn't have to say it was no fun: I think it was harder on him than it was on me.

When I finished and got his clothes back on, Dad thanked me. He still does this, whenever I tighten his belt or bring him his dinner or clip his fingernails. He's such a polite and decent guy, and his formality is so ingrained that I fear only death will end it—or possibly, extreme dementia.

Like many people, I'm intrigued by disaster: by the rampage of a tornado or tsunami, by a mountain lion that preys on bicyclists, by the electrifying *crump* of two cars colliding on the street. Or by people come undone in public: the woman screaming in front of the library steps when I lived in Boulder, Colorado, or the guy who unloaded his D9 dozer north of town and flattened the house his wife had taken in their divorce.

The disaster underway in this house is my father's dementia. Sometimes it crushes me to see his mind giving out, but other times I watch the process with morbid fascination. There's an element of drama, even glee, in how I report it. The storm is building, the crash is coming, and I want to see how far this will break down my father's reserve. He's been through plenty in life and stood firm. He maintained his composure in the face of my mother's affairs, her departure, and her death ten years later. He stood up to the chaos of his second marriage and a second painful divorce. In this last year he has endured, with never a complaint, Jane's decline and death. But now dementia is breaking him down. He's losing control, and there are times I'm not just fascinated by this earthquake of a disease, I almost root for it.

How can I have written that? Only hours later I'm ashamed and take it back, because Alzheimer's is making him miserable. When I try to get him ready for a walk, he can't find the sleeves of his coat with his flailing arms. He doesn't want his usual hat and jerks his head away when I start to put it on, a childish look of dread on his face. He seems to have forgotten the whole process of going outdoors. Watching him cling to his walker with such fear and hesitation, all I want is my constrained and lovely old dad.

After dinner it continues. He lies down on his bed and calls me in. There's something he wants me to do, but he can't say what it is. "The third floor," he says finally. "The people there have to push it up . . . and the people above must pull . . . and . . . and . . . " He can't find the words to explain it, and his face contorts in the despair of forgetting. "*Oh Jesus,*" he says. These are not words I grew up hearing from my father. He is so unhappy.

Looking through books on Dad's shelves, I find several references to his work and character. *Life,* in the early forties, brought the war into everyone's home. There had never been such graphic and immediate coverage of combat, and circulation grew, eventually topping five million, until *Life* became the country's most influential and widely read magazine.

Loudon Wainwright, in his book about the magazine, calls my father "a handsome, bright, reserved, efficient fellow," both "ambitious and proud," and marked from the start for bigger things. He calls him "cool and sensible."

In his diary, *Life*'s first editor, John Shaw Billings, calls my father "a mulish young Yankee" and "a stubborn little New England cuss."

Tom Prideaux, the entertainment editor, writes that "he never seemed motivated by the desire to show off or disport himself conspicuously. He didn't have an arrogant bone in his body. Yet there was nothing at all self-effacing about him."

At most magazines, the managing editor rides lower on the totem pole than the editor. Luce, as editor in chief, ultimately controlled all his magazines, but week to week at *Life* it was the managing editor who ran the show. In my father's three years at the helm, *Life* was in perpetual flux, trying to settle its focus. The war years had been simpler, with the bulk of every issue focused on the worldwide conflagration—and now, occasional arguments flared between Joe Thorndike and Henry Luce. In late 1948, after a "*Life* Goes to a Party" story about a dissolute ball in Honolulu, with photos of drunken, half-dressed party-goers, Dad received a twelve-page memo from Luce in which he announced that the managing editor "should never settle a dubious question of taste without concurrence of at least one senior colleague." At that, Dad promptly raised the question of whether he should continue at the magazine. Just as quickly Luce retreated, admitting that he had sent "a hastily-written document." But their relationship had begun to deteriorate, and only a month later Dad submitted a letter of resignation. "Effective today," it noted—though he added the escape clause, "unless you have any reasons to the contrary."

The two of them worked through that crisis as well, but on August 5, 1949, after reading a company memo from Luce that Dad felt undermined his authority, he made it clear he was finished: "I took this job on the understanding that I would have full authority and responsibility under your direction to run the magazine. . . . Last winter I submitted a tentative resignation, for the purpose of finding out where I stood. Lest there be any misunderstanding, this one is final and not subject to further discussion."

That same afternoon he cleared out his desk and took the train out to Connecticut. He'd had quite a run during his fifteen years with Time-Life, but by then he was ready to start his own projects. Eight months later, along with Oliver Jensen and James Parton, two friends from *Life*, he started a small publishing company called Picture Press. They did a book on cowboys with photos by Leonard McCombe and a commemorative book for Ford Motor Company on its fiftieth anniversary. Their major projects were the magazines *American Heritage* (described by the *New York Times* as "the most ambitious attempt yet made to merge readability with historical scholarship"), which appeared in 1954, and the expensively printed *Horizon* in 1958. Dad never made his million dollars—not by the age of twenty-five, or even at fifty-five when *Heritage* sold to McGraw-Hill—but for the rest of his working life he was his own boss and followed his own interests.

Ada Feyerick calls while he's taking a shower. She worked for him at *Horizon* and went on to write several books, and now she's aghast when I tell her he has Alzheimer's, that he's deeply forgetful and may have trouble placing her.

"This is terrible," she says. She can't get over it. "What a mind he had. Oh, I can't believe this. He was my mentor, he was a giant in the field—do you know what a giant he was?"

I do know this, a little—but it's lovely to hear Ada say it. I ask her to call back in forty minutes, and I talk to Dad about her as I help get him dressed. His face brightens at her name, and he says he remembers helping her with her first book. But he also thinks they worked together at *Life,* decades before he actually knew her. When she calls again I talk to her briefly, then pass the telephone headset to my dad. The headset always disorients him, but it's our only cordless phone. I settle the earpiece over his ear, and he smiles to hear her voice. Though Ada does most of the talking, he's friendly and enthusiastic, my old father all the way.

A line jumps out at me from Annie Ernaux's book about her mother and Alzheimer's, *I Remain in Darkness:* "Letting her stay at my place would have meant the end of my life. It was either her or me."

And from the same book: "Now when I come to see her, I'm still young. I have a love life. In ten or fifteen years' time, I'll still be coming to see her but I too shall be old."

A love life. As long as I stay with my father that seems impossible. Will I even want one, when all this is over? Instead I think of going to see Janir in Colorado, and taking a canoe trip with Barry. I could go to France with my old friend Elisabeth and sit in a café in her native town and write postcards, and relearn some French, and do nothing at all.

Even after his retirement, my father's life has been filled with writing projects. He has researched and written articles about one of his forebears who was hanged at the Salem witch trials, about Thoreau's trips to Cape Cod and down the Merrimack and Concord rivers, and about the nineteenth-century Transcendental utopia, Fruitlands. He wrote a futuristic novel, never published, about saving the human species. He outlined plans for a magazine devoted to the outdoors, and wrote a series of personal essays, some a bit pessimistic but none cantankerous, about the twenties, the economy, the natural world, population, and the century to come.

Twenty years ago he began research for his book about the Atlantic coast. He read through a long bibliography of reference works and popular history, and visited a thousand miles of coastline from West Quoddy Head, Maine, to Key West, Florida. In his desk I've found audiotapes of his interviews with harbormasters and coast guard officers, blueberry pickers and the head of Maine's Island Institute. He worked on the book for ten years, and it was published when he was eighty: "An effective combination of eyeball observation, rich history, and sad acknowledgment of how poorly we have used still another national resource," said *Kirkus Reviews*.

With that book finished he considered other subjects, expanding his files with clippings and notes about archeological digs, boat trips up the Amazon, the rise of the oceans and the disasters that will follow. But now, in these last few months, all his projects have fallen away. The work he loved is gone, and I think he's crushed not to have it.

At midday I carry a chair outside and set it on the gravel drive. Dad comes out and sits on it, wrapped in a sleeping bag, wearing his dark glasses and watching the birds at the feeder. I rake the drive and sweep the garage, soaking up a bit of the March sunlight.

Harriet, who will be working at a school camp in the White Mountains for a couple of weeks in April, brings over a friend who might be able to fill in for her, a barrel-chested Irish Bostonian named Jack Lane. He has a ruddy face, a watch cap over his balding head, two bad knees repaired last June, an easy way with words and lots of experience taking care of people. I like him from the start, though I know my father will have to get used to someone who talks as much as Jack does. When he leaves, he takes Dad by the arm and says, "You take care, Buddy."

That's how it goes with my father. He does not reach out and touch anyone, but some people take hold of him. It's hard to know when this is all right with him, and when he'd rather that all of us—including me—kept our hands to ourselves.

I've worried about a pair of recent attacks my dad has suffered, small crises that left him short of breath and immobile for thirty minutes at a time. These have baffled both me and Harriet—but ninety minutes after describing them to my father's general physician, Dad and I were on our way to Cape Cod Hospital for a CT scan and a better look at his lungs.

First some blood work, then they fed some dye into a vein and passed him through the large white donut. We waited. Someone saw something he or she didn't like on the film, and sent us over to the ER, where after three long hours in the waiting room we were admitted to the inner sanctum. Waves of orderlies and nurses, another registration, Dad in bed in a gown under some covers. Finally a doctor came in. He was moving fast but gave us the direct story. There was a pleural effusion—fluid in the sac surrounding the lungs—and also a small nodule. "I have to tell you, it may be lung cancer. If it is we'll call for radiation."

This was followed by more blood tests, antibiotics, an EKG and some prednisone. But to the doctor's dire announcement I saw little reaction from Dad. With his eyes hooded and his mouth turned down, he didn't look happy—but after all, by then we'd been in the hospital for six hours, and he hadn't looked that happy before the doctor came in.

After everyone left the room I talked it over with Dad. I said the words *lung cancer,* but he did not respond. He barely nodded. He doesn't want any part of what lies ahead: an appointment with a pulmonologist, then possibly more treatment and more time in the hospital.

His companion, Jane, died of cancer. She'd been treated for it, then told she was cured. At least that's what she reported to me: "All better," she told me a couple of years ago. "Clean bill of health." But when some symptoms returned she refused to go back for more treatment, and my father shares her view of hospitals. It's the last place he wants to go—and I don't want to be in the position of forcing him. *Could* I force him?

Nine hours after leaving the house that morning we pulled back into his drive. I fixed a quick dinner and we ate in silence. After his ice cream I asked Dad if he'd rather spend another day like this one, or a night with the shells flying overhead in a foxhole at Anzio.

"Anzio," he said.

Twice a day, as he has done for decades, Dad takes three inhalations of a preventive medication for asthma. But recently he's been having trouble with the inhaler. I've upset the routine by trying to get him to breathe the mist in deeply, rather than simply spraying it in his mouth while he locks up his chest.

I sit beside him as we rehearse the steps: breathe out, press the inhaler, breathe in and hold it. This simple operation has become a frightening ordeal. He knows he gets it wrong, and sits beside me with his eyes darting between me and the inhaler. When he does breathe in he can hold it for an amazing length of time, clamping the inhaler between his lips and looking at me as if to ask, *Is this right?* These are the moments that weaken me, when he looks most helpless and afraid.

His confusions grow worse. He's forgotten that Al and Ellen are on vacation in New Zealand, and thinks they'll be coming down from Vermont tomorrow. He thinks it's early morning and time for his shower, when in fact I'm cooking dinner. He needs to look again at certain boxes of papers, at his checkbook stubs, at a book about the brain written by Jane's daughter, Susie. He doesn't read it, but carries it with him everywhere. Yet always he's the same gentle guy. I'm still waiting for the changes in personality, the anger, the frustration erupting into violence. I want to say, I *knew* he wouldn't be like that.

But what will I do if he has lung cancer, and the doctors want to treat it?

I talk to LL about this, Janir's wife, who's a doctor in her first year of residency. "Why would you do that?" she asks. "For what? To get him back to where he is now? Radiation is hard on someone his age. It's hard on anyone. I wouldn't put him through it."

I talk to Harriet, who's even more definitive. "*Absolutely not,*" she says. "Only palliative measures. Keep him comfortable, treat pneumonia or other problems, but no radiation, no chemo, none of that."

In forty years of nursing, Harriet has seen it all. I'm glad to have her and LL on my side, because I fear the juggernaut of heroic medical care. It does no good to consult my father about any of this. Though his shortness of breath wears him down, I think he's lost all ability to weigh the odds, to evaluate the benefits of a hospital stay, to consider that some medical attention might alleviate his symptoms. Given the choice, no matter his condition, he would always want to stay home.

I rarely pass a day now without writing something down about my father. I came here hoping to look after him as long as I could hold out—and now I think I'll write about him for the rest of his life. He's ninety-one, he has Alzheimer's and asthma and atrial fibrillation, and now perhaps cancer, and I can't imagine he will live for another year. But my stay, this journal, and the end of his life now seem inextricable, each with some influence over the other. *Don't die*, I sometimes think, because I'm not finished writing about you.

The pulmonologist, Lawrence Pliss, soothes both of us. He slows down, he explains everything, he has a sense of humor, he covers all the options. It might be cancer, he says, but he doesn't think so. Dad hasn't smoked in sixty years, and then it was only for a year at the office. More likely, Pliss suggests, it's congestive heart failure. He asks us to go over to the hospital and have an x-ray taken. After that he'll either tap the lung from behind and withdraw some of the fluid or wait to see if Lasix will take care of it. Lasix is a diuretic that helps drain the body of the excess fluid that builds up with CHF.

Congestive heart failure: a condition marked by weakness, edema, and shortness of breath, caused by the inability of the heart to maintain adequate blood circulation in the peripheral tissues and lungs.

The hospital is just down the street from Pliss's office, and Radiology takes us right away. I sit on a bench as a pretty young nurse walks my father down the corridor to the x-ray machine, giving me a glimpse of how he must appear to others: a bent old man with rundown shoulders and unruly white hair, shuffling along with six-inch steps. My father, of course, is polite to this woman, and she is friendly to him. But I doubt that she can see the young man in him. When watching other old people, I can't do it myself. What would lead me to imagine that this old woman loved to dance the rumba, or that old man once ran the high hurdles, or that some stiff old couple once trekked through Nepal together? The older they are—and no one in the hospital looks older than my father—the harder it is to think of them as having once been young and supple and audacious.

I want to tell the young nurse about the summer day in 1955 when Marilyn Monroe showed up at our house to go waterskiing.

That was a big year for Marilyn. *The Seven Year Itch*, her twenty-fourth movie, had just been released, along with the iconic photo of her skirt blowing up above a sidewalk vent. What legs on that dazzling blonde, and what a smile.

My father had long been friends with Milton Greene, who was both photographer and friend to Marilyn, as well as an occasional business partner. Marilyn was spending the weekend in Connecticut with Milton and his wife, and mentioned to them that she wanted to try out the new sport of waterskiing. So Milton called my dad. We lived on Long Island Sound and had a little boat, though the motor was barely strong enough to pull a skinny twelve-year-old out of the water. I was twelve and, disastrously, had gone off with a friend for the day. But Dad knew someone with a bigger boat. Charlie Goit leapt at the chance, and Milton, Marilyn and a small retinue drove over to our place.

I wish I knew, or Dad could remember, what she wore and what she said, and every little detail. All I really know is that someone had to get into the chest-deep water with Marilyn and help her with her skis and keep her from tipping over until the line drew taut. And that was my father.

Up she surged, then crashed. Charlie circled around, Dad held Marilyn, and off she went again. On the third try she skied for a hundred yards, and Charlie got to haul her into the boat. But when I came home that evening the detail I heard from friends, neighbors and family, over and over, was how Charlie had to drive while my father stood in the water with his arms around Marilyn Monroe. I think everyone liked the irony of that, because Charlie was kind of lascivious, and my father more of a gentleman.

Fifty years later, walking down a hospital corridor with a pretty girl, my father has become a very old man. But he has some stories.

And tonight, over dinner, I ask Dad what he remembers of that summer day in 1955. Though he can't come up with many details, his version of the waterskiing seems pretty close to my own. He isn't sure about the bathing suit, but yes, most likely a two-piece. I admit to leading him some. And yes, he had his arms around her. "Around her waist," he says.

After that I can't help teasing him. "So someone had to get in the water and help out?"

"That's right."

"And that person wound up being you."

"Well, Charlie had to run the boat."

"And before you knew it, your arms were around her waist."

Deadpan, with only the faintest twitch of his eyebrows, "No alternative, really."

Dad isn't happy with Jack Lane. He doesn't remember his name, but calls him *the guy who talks too much*. Though it's true that Jack can gab, he's sensitive to Dad's position. "This is your father's sanctuary," he says, "and I'm the intruder here."

I keep thinking Dad will come around, as he did with Harriet. I hope he will, because she's about to leave for two weeks at her camp, and without Jack I'll have no help. A Friendly Visitor program from the Council on Aging has fallen through, as well as assorted respite care from Elder Services. After an interview and extensive paperwork, I might get a miniature grant for an eight-hour break planned weeks in advance. But what I really want is what I have now: two or three hours in the library every day, and two outings of tennis a week at the club I've joined. That ensures my sanity, and we have the money to pay for it. The problem is that except for Harriet, Dad doesn't want anyone to come over.

Am I coddling my father? My friend Elisabeth writes from Montreal:

> I think you should absolutely leave your dad
> sometimes for a few days in that home you visited.

You would be sure trained people would take care
of him, he wouldn't die for a stay of a few days
and he would probably care more about you when
you take him back home. He would probably
be angry at first but inside he would understand
that you need a bit of a life and that he is lucky
to have you. Don't feel guilty about this.

But she also understands how my father would hate to live in
one of those homes that look, as she says, "like a waiting room
for death."

I think if I put my father in a place like that he'd be dead in
three weeks, and I don't want that. I don't think I'll want it until
he does. Though many of his friends have now died, he never
talks about their deaths or says a word about his own. He wants
to live, and while I sometimes feel trapped in his house, and in
his life, I still want to give him what he wants.

From bedroom to bathroom and back again, that's his
only trajectory. "I'm a pissing machine," he told Harriet yesterday.

If a lifetime of strictures on his speech can fall away, I wonder if in the end he'll come around to welcome being rubbed, or
even held. Annie Ernaux writes, "Being alive is being caressed,
being touched." Not so for my father. But perhaps he must fall
back further toward childhood, to his early childhood, to whenever his parents last held him.

So many elemental facts of his life are lost forever. When did
his mother last hold him?

These days, in fact, he is touched more and more. Harriet
takes off his socks and kneels in front of him to rub lotion into
his ankles. When I come into the room she looks up at me like a
child who's getting away with something. The podiatrist buffs
Dad's nails, businesslike but with a feminine touch. Nurses

weigh him, take his pulse and blood pressure, hold his arm as he walks. I dress him. He doesn't like his shirt cuffs buttoned, so every time I put on his sweater his sleeves get drawn up around his soft biceps, and I have to reach up under his sweater sleeves, over his hairless forearms, and pull his shirtsleeves down. Somehow this feels more intimate to me than anything else I do.

The smallness of our days. Breakfasts and dinners at which we don't say a word. Nights when he's in bed by eight.

At three in the morning I wake, not suddenly but in stages. I must have had a dream but can't remember it. Outside, the lawn glares white with snow under a setting moon. Will this winter never end? But that's not it. Something large and overwhelming is wrong. Slowly it uncoils. My father is going to die, and I'm going to be alone.

He has been here always, every day of my life. He's falling apart but he's still my father, and once he goes I'm going to be left in a room in the middle of the night, in a house with a groaning furnace, and there'll be no meaning to any of it. So much will vanish when he's not in this world. It's four in the morning but I don't go back to sleep. I don't read or write, I just lie there missing him.

Easter morning, sunny and cool. Many are off in church today, but in my father's house we are keeping our own counsel. Dad is asleep, though he was awake earlier. Since no one is coming over today and there's nowhere we have to go, I've decided to let him choose when to get up. Every other morning I appear downstairs with a cheery greeting and an offer to heat up the bathroom. But all offers are coercive, and for once I'm not making any.

It's ten o'clock but I'm letting him sleep. Most days that's what he does anyway: he eats breakfast and goes back to bed, to sleep or simply lie there. I've also decided to try Sandy's regime, and bring Dad food only when he asks for it.

Noon. In Florida Terri Schiavo is living without food or water. In Rome the pontiff comes to his window but is too ill to speak. On Cape Cod I have corralled my father on one of his passages to the bathroom and given him his medications. His heart rate and blood coagulant level will stay under control, and the Lasix will continue to flush his system. For now the house is still, and Dad goes on sleeping.

I debate every step of this. Will he never ask for something to eat or drink? He's supposed to take plenty of fluids, but it's always been a struggle. If a patient is unconscious you just dump the liquid down the tube, but each day I must convince my fully conscious and resistant father to drink a glass of juice or water, then another and another.

My poor dad, up and down, back and forth to the bathroom as the Lasix wrings him dry. I've set out some snacks on the dining room table, so each time he passes he might see them. No interest so far. I haven't said anything about taking a shower or changing his clothes. It's two in the afternoon. The sun pours in through the newly cleaned windows, but Dad doesn't seem to notice the outdoors. He walks to the bathroom and returns to his room. He gets onto his bed, pulls the quilt up to his chin and lies there, still as a carving on a sarcophagus. He sleeps.

I'm going crazy, just watching him. I've tied myself to his day, to discovering what he wants. The whole debate about Terri Schiavo is over what she would have wanted for herself, and here on this formless Sunday it's clear that my father wants to lie in bed and not be bothered by anyone. He seems to have given up—but maybe that's what he has wanted all along. And if he wants to give up, doesn't he have the right to?

Three o'clock. How long will I let him go without drinking water? I've put two full glasses by his bed, but he hasn't touched them. I pace around the living room, I sit on the couch, I don't step outside into the beautiful afternoon. I sink with my father.

Five-thirty. The sun is going down, he looks exhausted and I can't stand it anymore. I'll make him drink something, then fix a dinner and set it before him. All offers are coercive, and so be it. But the question I've asked all day remains unanswered. Should I return to my jaunty self tomorrow morning and make him take a shower, make him change his clothes, invite him to sit down to his breakfast and morning medications, urge him to walk to the mailbox, insist on driving him to the ocean, hound him about drinking more fluids? At what point should I just let him do what he chose to do today: lie in bed without talking or moving.

I remember what the neuropsychologist said about taking Dad to the senior center: Don't ask him about it, just take him. I resist that, because Dad hates going over there. Yet today, on the one day I give him completely free rein, he winds up with no shower, no breakfast, no lunch, no time outdoors and no conversation. He's passed what seems to me a lost and unhappy day, stretched out on his bed.

And I have to ask: how much did I do this because I wanted a break myself, a day without responsibilities?

In the evenings, after I tuck Dad in, I've taken to sitting on his bed as he worries. His brow tightens, his voice quavers and his language drifts into scraps. I can never help him figure out what has gone wrong, or what he must do, but perhaps my presence makes it easier for him to give up the battle. Sometimes he simply drifts off. Other times he stops to signal his defeat. He sighs, he lets his eyes close and says in resignation, "Well, thank you."

Last night, sitting in the living room, I heard an odd mumbling from his room. I stepped to the door and found him pointing toward the foot of the bed. He couldn't speak. Instead he gurgled and groaned, with a look of consternation and a skinny finger jiggling in the air. I tried to figure out what he wanted, but couldn't. Was it the lamp? His hand wagged back and forth: *no no no.* Was it the dictionary? *No,* not that. His finger quivered and pointed toward—nothing, there was nothing there. I touched the curtain and he came out with a single clear sentence, "No, that's not it." But the next moment he was back to groaning, and no more words would come. His face drew tight with the effort.

This goddamn disease. There is always some new disaster and humiliation.

I moved my hands over the quilt. I touched the top of the wainscoting, and at that he spoke again: "That has to go."

"I don't think we can move this, Dad. It's part of the wall. We have to keep the walls."

He was calming down. He seemed to have recovered. He said "Good. Good. I just needed you to touch it."

Sometimes I wonder what I'm doing here—and then I imagine my father in a nursing home. Who would sit on his bed at night as he struggled with memory and order? How often would someone take him outside to sit in the sun? When would he have a dinner of ocean scallops and fresh asparagus? My dad would be the least demanding resident, and the last to complain. He'd just take what they gave him. I imagine visiting him in such a place, and how unhappy I'd be to see it.

I'm in the midst of giving Dad an emergency bronchial spray for one of his rare asthma attacks, when Jane's daughter Susie calls on the phone. It's not a good time to talk, but she promises to call back, and after dinner Dad waits by the phone.

Normally his interest in the phone is nil, but now he's going to wait beside it until it rings. It does and he picks it up. I don't know who it is, but Dad is abrupt. "I can't talk now," he says, and hangs up. It rings again, and he picks up the receiver. It's a call from Athens—I have ads in the paper, trying to find tenants for next year—and I get off the line as fast as I can. Ten minutes later, Susie.

What a smile she brings to his face. I don't think I've ever seen him beam like this, not with his children or grandchildren or anyone else. It's stunning, really. Months have passed since he last mentioned Jane's name, but every minute he's on the phone to her daughter his face is lit up.

After her call he's completely energized. He can't tell me what Susie talked about, but he sits at the table going through a *New Yorker*, an *Atlantic Monthly*, through the notebook in which Harriet records the details of her visits. Then he looks up and says, "Where's my money?"

"It's in your accounts."

"No, my money. What about the money that was spread out on the floor?"

"You mean dollar bills?"

"It was all over the place."

"Dad, I've never seen any dollar bills lying around. I would have picked them up."

"Well I want to see them."

He's still confused and upset about his joint checking account with Al, and I explain once again how that works.

"Is it my money, or is it Alan's?"

"It's yours, but he can spend some of it for you."

"Why don't the checks come to me anymore? I haven't seen them."

I explain about direct deposits. He wants to see the bank statement, and I have the latest one in a folder, ready to send to Al. But the statement now comes with a photocopy of the cancelled checks, and there he'll see the checks Al has been writing to me for staying here and looking after him. I'd rather he didn't see these, but he wants the statement so I hand it over.

He takes the statement and his checkbook into his room and sits down on the bed, and for forty minutes I hear the shuffle of pages. Finally he calls me in. "I can't make anything of this."

I reassure him. I tell him that after selling his house he has plenty of money. Most of it's in his mutual funds account, and he can spend it if he wants to, on whatever he chooses.

He listens. He considers. "What about you? You should be getting paid."

"I am getting paid." And finally I explain to him my arrangement with Al and Joe. "The fact is, *you* are paying me, a thousand dollars a week. It comes from your account."

His hand flutters up, then back to his checkbook. "You should be getting paid more."

This makes me wonder why I've been so secretive about it all along. "I'm getting paid plenty," I tell him, "and I'm really glad you've got the money for it."

I could say more about this. I could explain that I never completely escape the feeling that I should be doing this out of pure love. I know, by how seldom I mention it to other people, that there's something shameful about being paid for a job that so many others, in their own families, do for free. It doesn't matter that Dad, now that he's sold his house, has plenty of cash. Indeed, it could be said that he sold his house—something he didn't really want to do—so he could pay me to come live here. Money gets tricky fast with families and the elderly. While I know I'm doing a job no one else could do, it's awkward to put a price tag on it.

My doubts lift fast when the money arrives. I might be feeling desperate and shut in, worried about how long my life will put be on hold—but promptly, every two weeks, Al sends me a check for two thousand dollars, plus everything I've spent on food and household expenses. Save for a couple of years when I had some big movie advances, this is more than I've ever made in my life. I love these checks. I practically caress them before sending them off to my bank. I'm building up a wad to pay down my several mortgages, and I keep track of my checking account online, watching it as it grows. Just as Lois promised, money can take care of many discontents.

"Can I stay in my house?" my father asks.

"You'll always be able to stay in your house, Dad. You have three sons who love you, and we're going to make sure you don't have to go into a nursing home."

"I have that right, to stay in this house."

"You have that right, and we're going to defend it." I don't add any caveats.

In his file cabinet, alone in a manila folder, I find this penciled note in my mother's handwriting, on a simple piece of paper folded in three, with no date and no signature.

> Darling Joe—
>
> Thank you for your support. Your
>
> love, funny happy times—I shall miss you so—

The note has to be forty years old, and my father has kept it all this time. Can she have written this as she was leaving forever? I take it and show it to him.

"Do you remember this, Dad?"

Though he no longer wears his glasses, I believe he can still read. He holds the soft old sheet in his tremulous hand and studies it. "No," he says finally, and hands it back.

"That must be from my mother."

He looks straight ahead, not at me and not at the note I still hold between us. He has nothing else to say.

His mind is falling apart, and maybe he can't remember anything about the mother of his first two children. Maybe I've come across the note too late to learn anything about it from him. But there's no one else I can ask. I've pushed and goaded him before, and do it again. "This seems like a farewell note, but it's so short. It's not even signed."

He stares into the distance, looking like one of those residents I've seen in the dementia wings of nursing homes.

"I found this in your files," I tell him, "in its own folder. You must have kept it for a reason."

I'm dragging his past in front of him, one of his terrible losses. I'm relentless, I'm a shit, he would never do anything like this to me. But he has his defenses. He looks away. He says, "I don't know."

The trouble is, maybe he doesn't. Reticence and Alzheimer's have combined in him to make a perfect wall. I take the note upstairs, put it back in its folder and curl up on my horsehair mattress, frustrated and angry. At myself, at my father, at everything.

I think my mother left because it was so hard for my dad to open up. On the other hand, I'm sure they did have funny happy times, and he certainly supported her. When I was eight she went back to college, and after ten years became an anesthesiologist and began to practice. She had two boys, help looking after us, and a trustworthy husband—but she couldn't have found it easy to live with someone so contained.

Dad had plenty of quiet backbone. During the war he reported from North Africa, crossed the sea to Sicily where Patton was in command, and spent those nights at Anzio. After making his split from *Life* he took the risk of starting his own publishing company. He was ambitious and gentle and charming, and my mother had to love all that. But she also wanted an erotic life with some intimate talk.

They say children can spend a lifetime trying to repair the rift in their parents' marriage. It's a fanciful notion, but lying in bed in the early morning I sometimes think I'm doing exactly that. I think in some strange way I've *become* my mother. I imagine that if she'd lived she might have returned in my father's last days—even after years apart—and started looking after him, as I'm doing now. I see her kneeling down beside his bed and hugging him, as I would like to do. I see her weeping, as I would like to do. She stares at him, I stare at him, I don't know if I'm kneeling beside her or if I *am* her. My father lies asleep, his hand with the bent pinky clutching the sheet. His head has grown smaller, his hair is spiky, his chest slowly rises and falls. He's a lovable old man, and in their old age Mom doesn't care anymore about the romantic life she longed for when she was with him. She just wants to hold and reassure him.

It's my fantasy and I take it where I like.

My mother died in 1972, but how easily I come up with this scenario. Perhaps it's because when she was dying I didn't take care of *her*. I had my excuses, of course. I had a two-year-old son at the time, and a marriage in turmoil. My mother had been battling depression for ten years, and her craziness scared me, the depth of her losses. There was plenty of evidence of how much trouble she was in, but most of it I ignored, and then she was gone at fifty-seven. I was negligent, she died alone, and because of that I've always known that when the time came I was going to look after my father.

He's had a dream. "I had to walk," he says. "I had to go to the Athenaeum. And to the Old North Church, and the Old South Church, and to Boylston Avenue. I had to be there."

"Was there something you had to do?"

"I had to be there. I had to go to all those places. I think . . . now I have to go there."

He lies in bed staring up at the ceiling, then turns to me and asks, "Is any of this true?"

"Dad, I don't think so."

He watches me. Then, helplessly, "I guess it isn't."

For twenty-five years I've been coming to the Cape at the start of August. Al and his family are always here, sometimes Joe and his girlfriend—later his wife. Year after year I drive out from Ohio with Janir and a couple of his friends, or after he grows up and gets his license he comes on his own, driving down from his camp in Vermont with other counselors. His cousins bring their own friends and the house rings with laughter and noise. Every day at the beach we bodysurf, play volleyball and paddle tennis and heat-seeking missile. At night my dad cooks swordfish on the grill. The next generation wells up behind us, the kids are tireless, after dinner they shoot pool or play Ping-Pong or crowd around the dining room table for a raucous game of cards. These are the days my dad loves most, surrounded by his family.

But year by year his presence becomes less central. He retires earlier to bed. He comes to the beach for a shorter time, then not at all.

I have loved those summer days, but now can't imagine their return. I've absorbed my father's heavy heart and only want to be left alone. Spring, for which I've waited all these months, now grates on me: the cries of the baseball players on the diamond across the street, the *clink* of their aluminum bats, the first noisy families on the bike path, and the chattering high school girls who walk past on the sidewalk in their platform sandals, bare-toed in the cool sunlight. The world is rising but my father is going downhill, and I'm tied to his decline.

His conversation grows thinner. He can start a sentence, then something trips him up. "We have to see . . . ," he begins, and can go no further. It's a wrestling match with his memories, though I can't tell if it's the words or the thought itself that gets lost. Sometimes his eyes close and his mouth clamps down in a spasm of frustration. How I hate it myself when I can't remember someone's name, or when I have something to say and it vanishes. I want to stop everything until I pull it back. And this is what happens to my father all day long, every day.

David Shenk in *The Forgetting* tells the story of the famous patient known as H.M., whose hippocampus was surgically removed in an attempt to relieve his seizures. After that day he could remember his life from before the operation, but was unable to store new memories. "Time stopped for H.M. in 1953," Shenk writes. "For the rest of his long life, he was never again able to learn a new name or face, or to remember a single new fact or thought."

How miserable it must be to live without memories, without the complex bath of joy and regret and reminiscence, oblivious to all intimate ties once shared with others. Of course my father hasn't reached that stage. But if his body doesn't go first, it's what awaits him and every Alzheimer's patient.

Dad can spend thirty or forty minutes on the toilet, just sitting and waiting. I ask him if he's having any trouble. "I'm pissing," he says, sounding quite cheerful. "It's my only purpose in life."

Like Jane's death, or my mother's death, Dad never mentions his own. He never says anything like *when I die* or *after I'm gone*. I assume he's scared of dying, perhaps terrified, but I see no sign of that. As he gets closer to the end I'd like to hear some blazing revelation about what it's like to be approaching the great mystery—but nothing yet. He lies in bed staring. Sometimes he reminds me of how an infant gazes around the room, soaking things up.

Jane's daughter Susie drove up to visit my dad, which gave me a day off. I went to Boston and had dinner with a friend and his friends: lots of laughter and talk, and a powerful reminder that a social world is waiting, and someday I'll return to it.

Still, I was glad to pull back into Dad's drive that night, eager to see him and find out how his day had gone. I found him in the bathroom, bare-chested, and helped him put on his shirt. Susie, who was asleep upstairs, had left a note explaining that he'd gone to bed without a shirt, and she couldn't persuade him that he needed one. He looked rough: he hadn't shaved in three days, his breath was bad and he was confused. But there it was: I'd only been away ten hours and I'd missed him. I'd missed our small routines, and how polite he is, and how tightly I have to cinch his belt when I dress him, and the finicky way he picks up his fork and addresses his plate and spends fifty minutes eating dinner—everything that day to day gets under my skin.

After I tucked him into bed he lay still, looking up at me with both his good eye and his quavery, half-closed bad eye. "This is the night when everything is supposed to get dark," he said. "Unlike all the other nights."

I begged to differ. I said it got dark every night.

For a while he considered this, then nodded faintly. "Maybe so."

I felt a sudden pang. How much I'll miss him when he dies.

This morning Susie fills me in on their day together. He did fine, she says, he was lively and curious. They looked through some photos she'd brought, and a book on the *Life* photographers—and they talked. They talked about Jane, and even about Dad's marriage to my mother.

"He told me he wasn't ready," Susie says. "Apparently it was Virginia who wanted to get married, and he went along with it."

I've suspected this—but now he has talked to Susie about it! I feel cheated, I feel jealous. After all these months of looking after him, a woman steps in for one night and he spills his life story.

Yes, yes, it's not just some woman, it's his great and good friend's daughter, the closest he can come to Jane in the flesh.

But there's no fighting jealousy with logic. I feel abandoned. I've moved my life to my father's house, I've been here for months and he's never said *anything* about my mother. I bring up her name and he doesn't respond. I ask him about her years in medical school and he can't remember. I ask him about her love of elegant clothes, and he has nothing to say. I ask him about the miscarriage she suffered when I was sixteen, and he looks past me. Yet Susie can get him to talk about how he wasn't ready to get married. I sit in my chair and stew over his betrayal.

After Susie leaves I e-mail Lois about her visit, and mention what my father told her. Thirty minutes later the phone rings.

"That got your goat, didn't it?"

"Lois. Yeah, it surprised me."

"*Surprised* you. How about pissed you off?"

"I guess it did."

Lois has suggested before that my anger is far too buried. "If you're not mad at your father for shutting *you* out," she says, "you ought to be furious at what he did to your mother."

"She did plenty to *him*," I say. "She's the one who fell in love with somebody else."

"He shut her out. As a woman, I'm telling you, I've gone out with guys like your father and I wanted to strangle them."

I happen to know that Lois occasionally goes grocery shopping in a T-shirt that says, *I'm Out of Estrogen, and I've Got a Gun.*

Lois, in fact, is not out of estrogen and doesn't have a gun, she just likes the shirt. But her opinions are set about my father. "I've met him," she reminds me, "and I thought he was delightful. He was considerate and friendly and I can see how he charmed everyone. But he was cold to your mother. That drove her out and she killed herself because of it."

With this she has gone too far. She only met my father once, when he and Jane came to Santa Fe for a visit, and my mother died years before that. "He didn't drive her out," I say, "he just didn't give her everything she wanted." By now I have my coat on and I'm walking around outside, because whether Dad can hear me or not, I can't talk like this inside his house. "He wasn't raised to be affectionate," I say in his defense. "He didn't have it in him."

"Of course he had it in him. He *chose* not to let your mother in, just as now he chooses not to let you in."

Lois and I argue easily, with no rancor left at the end of the day—but at times like this she can sink her teeth into the facts. "Look how he talks to Jane's daughter," she says. "He'll open up when he wants to, he just won't open up to you."

I start to speak, then stop. I can't deny this.

"You're upset about it, so imagine how angry your mother might have been. He judged her and found her lacking. He walled her out. He walled out his second wife, too. But not Jane. He loved Jane."

"He loved my mother."

"I know you want to think that. But I wonder. The way you describe your dad now, he's the same cold guy. The way he thanks you for everything, like you're an employee. Never saying he loves you, never touching you. Is he even glad you're there?"

"Of course he's glad. Otherwise he'd be in a nursing home."

"If he's glad, describe that to me. Does he love having you there? Does he take pleasure in it?"

I'm still wandering around on the lawn. Across the road a baseball team has taken the field, and someone is hitting fly balls and line drives to the outfielders, the high ring of the bat sounding out from home plate. I have to admit that Dad seems neutral about me. I take him to the beach and the doctor's office, I cook for him, I dress him, I read to him—and he goes along with my attentions. We talk, occasionally he smiles, but he never seems curious about what I think or feel, or asks anything about my life outside his house.

"His dementia has to be part of it," I say. "He's disappearing into his own world."

At this Lois softens. "I'm sure this is a hard time for him. He's lost so much, it must be hard to think about anything else."

Her analogy—between how he treats me now and how he treated my mother when they were married—doesn't really hold up, because Dad was far more attentive to all of us back then, and much has changed with his dementia. But Lois has stirred up some memories. We talk for a while about her editing business and life with her husband, Wayne, but I'm greedy in wanting to talk about my father, and she's generous in letting me. I ask her, "Have I ever told you about my father and the cat?"

"You haven't."

"It was a big black and white cat with a hanging paunch that would jump onto my dad's lap whenever he sat on the couch. And once it did he wouldn't get up, he didn't want the cat to be disturbed. It never occurred to me that instead of being so considerate of the cat, he could have shooed it off and sat around with my mother instead. You know how it is when you're a kid—whatever goes on in your house, you think that's the way life is. Then, when I was a freshman in college, my mother gave me a copy of Lawrence Durrell's *Justine*."

Lois knows the book. It's a novel set in Alexandria, Egypt, a luxuriant story of sex, love and intrigue. My mother read it before passing it on to me at eighteen, a Faber & Faber paperback with her checks and brackets in the margins, and some notes in her tiny hand. My father wouldn't mark a book, but my mother wrote right on the page. I wish I still had that paperback. It was lost years ago in a hurricane, soaked through in the basement of my father's house, and I've forgotten most of my mother's comments. But one I can still see, in pencil near the top of the page on the left-hand side: "He pays more attention to the cat than he does to me."

A long pause from Lois. "She wanted you on her side."

"I was always on her side."

That year, though I didn't know it, my mother was in the midst of a four-year affair. She was in love with another man, and in retrospect I can see how she was explaining herself to me, even justifying her adultery, by giving me a novel that celebrated everything she couldn't share with my father. The book was a map of my mother's emotional and sexual interests, of all the topics that never came up in our house. She had put a check next to this passage:

> Certainly she was bad in many ways, but they
> were all small ways. Nor can I say that she harmed
> nobody. But those she harmed most she made
> fruitful. She expelled people from their old selves.

Two years later my mother would expel my father, expel all of us from the protective shell that had been our family. I would be torn, because I wanted my family to stay together, but I understood my mother's drive for what I craved myself, both tenderness and raw sex.

That was forty years ago. Looking back, the gulf between my parents' natures is clear, the discrepancy in what they hoped for in a marriage. My mother was the one who wandered, but both of them suffered. It was *Madame Bovary*, it was *Anna Karenina*. It was a train wreck—and for Alan and me, two kids in the caboose, the whiplash was inevitable.

In working my way through Dad's files, I discover an old letter from my mother to my father which pretty much confirms his take on who led whom to the altar. It's written on stationery from a New Hampshire hotel, undated, but from sometime early in 1939, shortly after my parents had begun to date. To sleep with each other, I would guess.

Darling—

If you only knew how happy I am. I'm all alone.
I arrived just in time to meet Jim Parton walking
out the door, so I had dinner at the Inn with him
and some friends, said goodbye to Mary Jane and
her Dutchman who is very sweet, and went to bed
about 8:30. I just have to be by myself sometimes,
and it does me a great deal of good. My soul is
simply flourishing. It's very quiet here, only two
other people at present. Probably that's because
the slope is so icy—there are only very small parts
that a novice can manage. I am being very careful
of 1) steep slopes 2) I am making fast stem-bogens
or is it bogens around blond ski instructors.

It's a marvelous vacation—nothing but
exercise, food and sleep. I guess I'm a very
elemental girl. It makes me ridiculously happy.
Thanks for inviting me to Florida—but I
just have the feeling this is right. It is.

I'm much more broadminded than you
are—have you also found a blond chorus girl
named—please—anything but Bunny? The hotel
sounds terrifying. Do you actually drink on the
sand or indulge or practice or celebrate Bingo
nightly? And if I hear of you being unfaithful to the
little green boat, all hell is going to break loose.

My last week in town was not a bit what I
expected. I think everybody assumed that I
would be lonely and did his best to prevent it.
My family planned this and that . . . and Alex,
doing his bit, took me to lunch, where we met
up with Bucky Fuller and Isamu Noguchi. So
the next night Noguchi (statues: AP bldg), Alex,
Mrs. King II and I all went to see "Juno—the

Paycock." I don't know whether you'd classify this type of theater as culture or education.

But I enjoyed it very much—and it was excellently done. You should have seen Noguchi laugh when I showed him how I could look Japanese. (Have you ever seen it? All I have to do is hold up the corners of my eyes a little.) I can look much more Jap than he can.

Darling I miss you very much—not that you will believe it. Next week I will be very happy.

Love, Virginia

The little green boat? Alex King had written for *Life*, then edited the magazine *Stage*, where my mother worked as an editor. Isamu Noguchi was a well-known Japanese American sculptor who did many statues and gardens in the U.S., Europe and Japan, and whose workshop in Queens is now a museum.

My mother at the time was an assistant photo editor at *Life*, twenty-four years old, recently divorced from Larry Tidball, a truck driver she'd married because, as she once told me, "I thought I'd never get another offer." In 1937, after three years of marriage, they'd moved from Columbus, Ohio, to Beaumont, Texas, where she took a job as the host of an early talk-radio show. Larry, a jealous man who didn't think his wife should be working, used to call her up at the station and use a disguised voice to ask her out on dates. After six months in Texas—a state she hated for the rest of her life—she'd had enough. She packed two suitcases with her best clothes and took the train to Brooklyn, where her father had found a job teaching music. It was supposed to be a visit, but she once confided to me that she had tucked her diaphragm into one of her suitcases. She didn't plan to go back to Larry, and eventually admitted this to her parents. Her father put his arm around her and said, "Ginny, there's nothing you have to do, as long as you're willing to pay the price."

Other than these few details I know nothing about her first marriage. Larry Tidball is dead, and though I've tracked down some members of his family, no one knows anything about my mother. They've never heard of her. It's amazing how much has vanished.

Only a couple of years later she was writing that crafty letter to my father, replete with stories of lunch with Bucky, the theater with Isamu and collisions, possibly dangerous, with those blond ski instructors. Yes, I'd say she was reeling my father in. Dad was an editor at *Life*, and Mom an underling, but I doubt if he was half as wily. And of course I have to root for her: we're talking about my existence here!

A week ago Dad told me he wanted to go down and see Oliver Jensen again in his nursing home. I phoned Dotty Turner, a woman who visits him almost every day, and found that Oliver isn't doing well. He's eating less, he rarely speaks, he can't stand up, and when they stretch him out on his bed he soon curls back into a fetal position. About the only thing he seems to enjoy is when Dotty reads to him from his own book, *Carrier War*, the one I took him last fall. I told my father all this, but left the implication unsaid, that Oliver is close to the end.

In a lucid moment a couple of days later Dad announced, "I'm going to talk to the obituary editor at the *Times* about Oliver. I have to put something together, with dates and people. His family won't do anything."

On a personal level my father rarely speaks critically of anyone. But when it comes to Oliver's family his reserve breaks down. "I don't think they care. They don't know anything. You ask them what he wrote and they say, *some books.*"

I was leery of taking Dad on a seven-hour round trip, and in the end persuaded him that the drive was too long for him. I would go myself, I told him. I didn't explain that one reason I wanted to go was to see what might lie ahead for the two of us.

The next night after dinner I set my tape recorder on the dining room table. "How about saying a few words to Oliver?"

"In this? What do I do?"

"Just talk. It's already recording."

He was silent a long time. I took the dinner plates into the kitchen and washed them, and only after turning off the water heard him start, slowly at first, then warming to his message:

> Hi, Oliver, this is Joe Thorndike. I couldn't come down to see you today because they put me in the hospital. For no good reason, but they did. Now I'm happily back home again. I had hoped to come down to see you, but it doesn't look as if I could, because it's such a long trip down there, and I've pretty much decided to stay on Cape Cod. I'm living in Harwich now and wish I could see you, but I guess they think I better not make such a long trip at this point. I'm mostly in the hands of my son John, who's looking after me and telling me what I can do and what I cannot do, and so far it's working out very well. So anyway, I send you my very best when he sees you. And one of these days I'll see you again, and we'll renew old times and old acquaintances.

My father can really pull it out of a hat. I'm sure he hasn't spoken that many words in a row since I came last December. When I transcribe them I come close to crying: old times and old acquaintances. Of course they were far more than acquaintances. In addition to being friends for over sixty years, they were the editorial engine for both *American Heritage* and *Horizon,* and for dozens of large illustrated books on American and world history, on art, culture and archeology. My father wrote a pair of those books—*The Magnificent Builders* and *The Very Rich*—and Oliver wrote others: *The American Heritage*

I'll be taking down some old photos of the two of them, some long letters from Oliver proposing various articles, and assorted office memos that go back to their days at *Life.* In one of these my father has asked Oliver to write a short piece about "a girl washing a dinosaur," for which they have some photos. Oliver, well known at *Life* for his humorous memos, typed in a response below Dad's message: "We lost all the pictures so I had some new ones taken. Through an oversight they show the dinosaur washing the girl, but I still feel this is a noteworthy subject, of interest to our readers."

Oliver's room is as clean and sunny as before, and Dotty is there waiting for me. She's Oliver's one steady link to his past, to the years before he moved into this home. She used to keep house for him, and after he stopped driving she often took him around to see the trains, of which Oliver has long been an aficionado. They'd sit and talk and watch the Amtrak coaches roar by, or stop in at the Essex Steam Train, the tiny railroad line Oliver helped rescue from extinction. Today, inside his room, there's no sign that Oliver ever had any interest in trains.

As Dotty has warned me over the phone, he's shrinking. His white hair still stands up tall, but he lies half-curled and belted onto a kind of chaise on wheels. His eyes look unfocused and he grinds his teeth, loudly and without pause. It's a war of molar on molar, and sounds like the end of the world. It's hard to believe that after a week of this he'll have any teeth left.

I think he still remembers my father. At least his face breaks into a smile when I play Dad's tape. But only halfway through the message he begins to fidget and move his legs from side to side. "I can't figure this out," he says, plucking at the belt that holds him down. By the time I pull out the letters he wrote to my dad, he has begun his litany: "I have to get out of here."

I glance at Dotty, who has cared for Oliver throughout his decline—"I loved the man," she will tell me later—and see how close she is to tears.

On the wall is a montage of Oliver snapshots, taken with Dotty and various attendants at the home, almost all of them women. Just as I'm thinking that women are the usual attendants not only of birth but death, into the room strides a handsome young woman from somewhere in the French-speaking islands. It's clear, as she bends close to his face, that Oliver has charmed her as well. "How you doing, Ah-lee-ver? *Bonjour, bonjour. Comment allez-vous? Ça va?*" She turns to us with her glorious smile. "He is a good man, *Olivier Jensen.*"

Her radiant spirits, I think, could float a hundred sinking patients, and me with them. She speaks more French to Oliver, she arranges his restive legs and ignores his grinding molars. She gives him her full attention for three or four minutes, then says, "Okay, I'll let you be with your people."

"They're interesting people," Oliver says.

"Yeah, they are. See you later, Ollie dear. *Au revoir.*"

But as soon as she leaves, Oliver begins again: "I have to get out of here. I can't make head or tail out of this." His legs, long and thin, rise into the air, then fall. "I have to go. I need to get out of this building. Help me leave, I have to leave here."

That's his one ambition, and he's unhappy about being tied down. Dotty can usually calm him. She tells him he has to be patient, and he's patient for a minute. She tells him the truth—"You can't leave, Oliver," and, "You have to stay here"—and she also tells him what must be small lies: "When it gets warmer I'll take you for a drive. We'll go see the trains."

He grinds his teeth, and I'm glad my father hasn't come. I'm not reassured about what lies ahead for Dad, but on the drive home console myself with a picaresque detail that Dotty reported as Oliver napped. For a couple of weeks, after they'd upped his Aricept from five to ten milligrams, he became quite a problem with the attendants, with the nurses, even with Dotty.

"What did he do?"

"Oh, you know."

"What?"

She rolled her eyes. "Oliver thought he was sixteen again."

This makes me smile. See you later, Ollie dear. *Au revoir.*

Cape Cod can't seem to get on with spring. Barely a bud opening on any twig, and the high all week hasn't cracked fifty. This morning on NPR Ketzel Levine did a lyrical piece on the dogwood, and I was flooded with the loss of my Appalachian spring: loss of the shy dogwood, loss of the redbuds that dot the edge of my woods at home, their purple buds and flowers standing out against last year's dead leaves. If I were on my farm I'd be walking out to the pond with friends, breathing in the dense air, soaking up the season as if it were our last.

Every night I go through a few more of Dad's files, folder by folder. There are letters from my mother in the mid-sixties, explaining her depression and hospitalization. Letters from me when I was farming in Ohio and raising Janir on my own, and numberless photos of my mother: cute on skis, svelte coming off a diving board, sensual but faintly bucktoothed as a teenager.

My father, though he speaks so rarely about the past, has archived his entire history. There are boxes full of memos from his days at *Life* and *American Heritage*, genealogies prepared by his mother, newspaper clippings about islands off the coast of Maine, letters from Janir's mother, photos of the trip Dad took with Joe Jr. to Hadrian's Wall in England. Everything must be kept, yet none of it is consulted. Dad has collected all the evidence but never wallows in his own history. That's up to me.

Over the years, discovering my mother's history has also been up to me, including the details of her infidelities. This is a subject my father would not have discussed with her, so I probably know more about it than he does. When married to her first husband, I believe she was faithful. She told me she was, and at the start I think she was faithful to my father, too. Or was she? Was she going to bed even then with Isamu Noguchi, of whom she once told me, "I loved how he smelled, of sandalwood." Certainly at some point in her marriage she began to sleep with other men. I wasn't aware of this growing up, but on a trip through Guatemala—she had come to visit me when I was in the Peace Corps in neighboring El Salvador—she raised the topic. I think she was lulled by the beauty of Guatemala, by the volcanoes, by the hotel we stayed in overlooking Lake Atitlán, a hotel with a grand piano on which she played the piano part of Schubert's Trout Quintet. And lulled by the next hotel, in Chichicastenango, where we lay in beds under thick hand-loomed blankets on opposite sides of a fire in a whitewashed grate, talking late into the night. It was there she told me of the other men.

"There were several," she said.

I was not surprised. I already knew about one of them, and as soon as she mentioned the others they seemed inevitable. But as the fire settled to embers, it wasn't the others she wanted to talk about, it was the one who still mattered to her, the one I already knew about, the man who'd brought her marriage and our family to an end. He was a fellow doctor thirteen years her junior, an ambitious young Cuban who looked, as our friend Patty Coughlan once said, like a beautiful Tahitian boy. I'll call him Julio, and further the disguise by changing some details of his field of medicine. Some years later, after my mother died, I tracked him down on the phone. He was cautious but agreed to see me, and we set up an appointment to meet at his hospital in Miami. I had to go there anyway, to put Janir on a plane to visit his mother and grandmother in El Salvador, and when I stepped out of a cab at Julio's hospital my heart was still knocking around with the lonesomeness of watching my boy disappear into an airliner. I had a backpack, a full beard and hair to my shoulder blades. It was 1976.

I'd hoped to go out to dinner with Julio, but when I arrived at his office he shook my hand and sat down on the other side of his desk, still wearing his white lab coat. Twice Security poked their heads in the door, and twice they called on the phone. He obviously feared that as the son of the ruined woman I might turn vindictive and dangerous. I wasn't going to do that, or even question him too sharply, because I didn't want to scare him off. There was too much I wanted to learn, and for the first twenty minutes I listened as he sat, protected by his desk, and fed me pablum about how my mother had divided her life into different compartments, and he was in "the friends compartment." Finally I stopped him. I told him I knew about their affair, and quoted what she'd told me that night in Chichicastenango: "I had four years of absolute love, and it was worth any price." That softened him up and he began to talk—though not at first about himself. Perhaps protectively, he wanted me to know about her other men.

Her first lover, he told me, had been her diving coach when she was still in high school. It was an illicit and underage affair with a married man—but they had clearly remained friends afterward, because years later, as a teenager, I met the guy myself after he hired my grandmother to work as a social hostess at his hotel in the White Mountains. My whole family spent a week at that hotel with no hint, at least to me, that he'd ever been more than a coach to my mother. He sat by the pool and chatted with my parents, as Alan and I did cannonballs off the low board. His wife gave me a golf lesson.

What an actress my mother must have been. But as Julio talked I could feel the river that had run through her life, the desire she grew used to hiding. At seventeen I had barely kissed a girl, but my mother had been sleeping with a guy of thirty and keeping it under wraps.

I was confused to find that Julio was an internist. "I thought my mother told me you were a surgeon," I said. "No," he said delicately, "that was . . . your mother's friend before me." He named that surgeon, a man I'd heard her speak of fondly, and with whom she maintained a friendship until she died. He named Robert Capa as well, the *Life* photographer and famous womanizer. My mother had never mentioned Capa, but I'd heard about him through Patty Coughlan, who let slip some stories after my mother died.

Julio explained that she had tried to make all her affairs safe. Either the men were playboys like Capa, or married and not about to leave their families, any more than my mother was about to leave hers. Julio, who was married, was also supposed to be safe, but he wound up leaving his wife and children. During the hours we spoke he never echoed my mother's remark about four years of absolute love—he never mentioned love at all—but he confirmed what she'd told me, that they had planned to live together, had planned to marry, had rented an apartment in Miami and started to move in. Then it all fell apart.

I took most of what Julio said at face value, while aware that he might have been tailoring his stories. I don't know how honorable or truthful he was, but no matter: I wasn't looking for a guilty party. My mother had made it clear to me that the love she shared with him had been worth all the pain that followed, and that's what I wanted to hear about. Was her pain—and mine, and my brother's, and my father's—balanced by the passion she'd known with this man?

I couldn't see it in him. Perhaps it was his lab coat, or the slight stoop of his shoulders. Or perhaps he was shielding me from the power of their affair. In the thirteen years since he'd left my mother, he'd written "four books and a hundred and sixty articles" for medical journals. He worked too much, he admitted. He had married a second time, then divorced. We talked for two hours. I wanted to hear everything, and it was now or never. But while I learned a lot, I couldn't see what had so transported my mother about this man. There was a coolness to him, a slight weariness. Still, he opened up and told me a lot. With plenty of men in his position I would have hit a stone wall.

Before we finished, I asked him about his breakup with my mother. I didn't say what he must have known already, that the day he left her was the day she started to die.

My parents had separated only two weeks before. She'd waited until the last moment to tell Dad she was leaving—in fact she never did tell him, because only days before she was planning to depart, he asked, "Virginia, do you want a divorce?"

"I do," she said, and the decision was made.

In the years that followed she told many people, "Joe asked for the divorce." Shabby, I've always thought—though by then she was drinking steadily and padding her despair with Seconals and Darvons.

Here's the story I heard from her. Julio told a rather different story, but this is the one that rings true to me, given everything that followed.

I was in college and Alan at boarding school, and her new life was about to begin. She drove down to Florida in Julio's car to outfit the apartment they had rented in Miami, and spent a couple of sunny days buying sheets and towels, curtains and bedspreads, preparing their nest.

He arrived one evening before dinner. All this she described to me that same night in Chichicastenango, with the fire burning down in the grate. "He left his suitcase by the door, but I thought nothing of it. I had dinner ready, and later we went to bed. We made love. In the morning I got up and fixed our breakfast. A simple breakfast, just coffee and English muffins. I noticed that he'd dressed in the same clothes as the night before, and that he hadn't moved or unpacked his suitcase. Still, I had no idea. After he finished his muffins he set his napkin on the table and stood up. He said, 'Virginia, I have something to tell you. I've decided that I don't want to marry you after all.'"

At first she didn't believe him. They fought, she screamed and cried, but none of it did any good. His mind was made up, and a cleaver came down on her life. In the afternoon she took his car and began to drive, and to drink. She'd been a drinker before, she often had a cocktail before dinner, sometimes two, but nothing like this.

"I had no idea where I was going. I wandered in circles, I drove for twenty-four hours and wound up in Savannah, Georgia. I knew I'd kill myself if I stayed at the wheel, so I found the airport and flew to LaGuardia. But when I got out of the plane I had nowhere to go. I had no home, I had nothing. I couldn't go back to your father. I took a room at the airport hotel and sat on the bed shaking, afraid to go near the window because I thought I might open it and jump."

So began ten years of struggle with heartache, alcohol, depression and prescription drugs. There were other blows as well. She was forty-seven and soon entered menopause. Although she had weighed 118 pounds almost all her adult life, her weight jumped to 160. Her best friend, Jane Parton, died of cancer, leaving three small children. Her psychiatrist committed suicide. My father remarried and had another son.

After their breakup Mom stumbled along on her own. She fought to stay alive, she doggedly made new friends, she enrolled in a program to become a psychiatrist. The battle ended ten years later, two days after my thirtieth birthday, when she died on the floor of her New York apartment with a lethal quantity of drugs and alcohol in her tissues. There was no note, but the coroner ruled it a suicide. I call it that myself—but in fact, I don't think she was clear in her intent. I think she just wanted to be unconscious.

I'm glad that my mother started talking to me on that trip through Guatemala, and that later I tracked Julio down. My judgments about him seem insignificant next to what I learned about my mother. I only wish I knew more. I wish I knew everything. I am that strange guy who would like to see, through some magical *Truman Show* process, the complete video of my parents' lives, every delicate or searing moment. It seems clear to me that if I want to understand myself, I have to start with my mother and father.

Sometimes I wonder what would have happened if my mother had never slept with any other men, if she had restrained herself and settled for a domestic life. My family might have remained intact, and that might have been great for me and my brother, perhaps also for my father. But I have to consider, as my mother would, the price of such accommodation. Pinned above my desk at home is a card bearing the question asked by a character in James Salter's novel *Light Years.* "But isn't it better," Nedra asks her husband, "to be someone who follows her true life and is happy and generous, than an embittered woman who is loyal? Isn't that so?"

It's another conundrum with no easy answer, especially for a woman with children. For years my mother tried to avoid a decision, by remaining inside her family and finding passion elsewhere. Passion eventually crushed her—yet she had made her choice and stood by it. She had already suffered for years when she told me that the love she'd found had been worth any price. She never backed down from that claim, so I never dismiss her verdict.

My father, perhaps all along, had made his own choice about it. He stepped back and got out of the way. He must have known she was having affairs, but I don't think he ever said anything about them. Talking things over was beyond him, and the marriage collapsed. About their divorce I have never taken a side, nor did they ask me to. As Plato reminds us, everyone we meet is fighting a hard battle—and that was surely true of my parents. The guilty party, the one who ran off, was my mother. But I don't want all the blame to fall on her, I don't want to blame either one of them. I'm now the guardian of their marriage and divorce, and hold them to me as gently as I can.

Joe Jr. has published a spirited Op-Ed piece in the *New York Times* on tax day, April 15, which I read to my father over breakfast. While acknowledging that the tax code is incredibly complicated, Joe claims that in fact, "filing taxes is too easy, not too hard." A daring thing to say. But with TurboTax and paid preparers, Joe explains, we avoid the trauma of figuring out what we have to pay. "So why is this bad? When it comes to taxes, pain can be a good thing. It keeps people vigilant, encouraging them to keep a wary eye on government."

I'm not sure how closely Dad follows Joe's argument, but I know he's glad to see him published in the *Times*. All day he sits with the paper on his lap, folded open to the Op-Ed page. Success is lovely—and Dad bathes in it far more than if he'd written the piece himself.

He had a rough afternoon yesterday, short of breath when he lay in bed and dizzy when he walked to the bathroom. He didn't want any dinner—he never does—but setting the food on the table seemed to revive him, and he ate until his plate was empty.

We eat well here, better than either of us would on our own. Dad's evening meals last fall, when he was cooking for himself, were all fat-filled frozen dinners: pot pies, breaded fish sticks and cheesy lasagnas. Now, on his tab, I buy shrimp, cojo salmon, thinly sliced chicken breasts, fresh peppers and sweet potatoes. Harriet cooks clam chowder at home and brings it over in crocks, and I'm sure Dad's meals are a far cry from the bland-looking food I've seen at nursing homes.

But tonight, after his dinner, he sits across from me, sinking fast. His eyes are closed, he's having trouble with his stomach or chest, or possibly it's his throat, and every ten seconds he grunts quietly. His fists are raised to the edge of the table, and his head is tilted back. He holds his breath, lets it out with a moan, breathes in, holds it, grunts again. His face is contorted, yet when I ask if something is bothering him, he says no. No pain, he says, no problem of any kind. His face radiates misery but there's nothing wrong. He goes back to his steady grunting.

Later, as he lies on his bed, the grunting persists. Again, because I can't stand it, I try to figure out what's bothering him. "Is it your chest?" I ask.

"No."

"Is it your stomach?"

"No."

"Can you put your hand where it doesn't feel good?"

For a long time, nothing. Finally he lifts his bony right hand and touches his thumb to his pinkie, the one he can't fully extend. "It's here."

"You mean that's what's bothering you, your finger?"

"It's not really bothering me, I'm just aware of it."

That's all I can get out of him, and I go off to wash the dishes, scrubbing them obsessively, doing a job I can carry out to perfection.

"How rewarding it must be," someone told me the other day, "to look after your father."

Rewarding sounds pale and formal, because I'm far more engaged than that with my dad. I struggle when he does, I'm lifted up when he takes pleasure in something, and miserable when his day falls apart. I'm no longer disconnected from life and realize, looking back on the last four months, that I haven't once been depressed.

For most of my adult life I've suffered from bouts of depression. Though they're never so bad that I can't eat, sleep and work, they seem to drop in out of nowhere, and can be intractable. One day life is a thrill, and the next it's meaningless, nothing interests me, I plod along, I don't know what I'm doing on earth. But this year, though I've had some blue moments, full depression has vanished. I'm too busy, I'm far too wrapped up with my father to lose faith in the world.

A few days ago I wrote my friend Paul Kafka-Gibbons and told him I hardly care anymore about my dad's memory, I just don't want him to be anxious and troubled.

Paul wrote back: "It's like what people have told me about having kids with learning and development and behavior problems. You think you want them to be famous brain surgeons or something, and it turns out all you really want is for them to be happy and connected."

In the public eye, my mother was the mischievous parent, having torn up my family to go after the romance she wanted. My father was honorable but could not hold onto her. I understood her desires, but also worried that I'd wind up like him, and in my early twenties set out to change my nature and become the kind of man my mother wouldn't leave: someone open to sex, someone who could laugh and weep and expose the inner life my father kept hidden.

I couldn't have put this into words at the time, and barely knew what I was aiming for when I stepped out of academics into the hippie world, where people were having fun, and fucking, and looking each other in the eye. The sixties—most of which took place in the seventies—had arrived just in time, and instead of the old order of my parents' marriage, I headed for something new.

I met Clarisa Rubio when I was in the Peace Corps in El Salvador, a half-Mayan girl of nineteen who'd spent the last five years in San Francisco. After marrying we traveled, then lived in a tent at 7,500 feet above Boulder, then moved to Chile and bought a farm. Clarisa was the driving force, the one who impelled us to a primitive life. Going back to the land was a common adventure in the early seventies, but in southern Chile we took it to an extreme, living miles from the nearest small village. We had no car, no telephone, no electricity and no running water. And by then we had Janir, only two months old when we moved onto the farm.

Clarisa seemed to know everything about child raising. I'd read some books, mainly about kids and education: John Holt's lucid volumes and Joseph Chilton Pearce's *The Magical Child*. But I knew nothing about babies, having held only one in my life before Janir. Clarisa knew babies from her family and did not consult any books. When they told her in the hospital that she shouldn't feed her son for twelve hours after his birth, she put his mouth to her breast. He was hungry, he ate, and no one's theories were going to get in the way. We had no bassinet or crib or stroller. We had no bottles or formula, or any schedule. I was raised on a schedule, but Clarisa's way was to give her baby what he wanted. She nursed him, she carried him everywhere, she lay in the orchard with him for hours, laughing with him and playing with his toes. She picked him up by one foot and draped him over her shoulder. They spent all day together, and after dinner she took him to bed, where he nursed and they fell asleep, his skin still in touch with hers.

I held him myself, more and more as he grew, and when I got him at two and a half—as Clarisa sank beneath her rising schizophrenia—he was in and out of my arms all day. Our marriage hadn't rung in much of a new order, but my life with Janir did.

For weeks I've been sending Lois entries from my journal. "Am I paying attention to the right things?" I ask her in an e-mail. "Is it unfair to write about my dad's failings, at this debilitated stage of his life when he can make no response?"

Lois answers, "I can understand why you're afraid to look too close. You don't want to challenge him. The two of you are stuck together now, and it's all too late anyway. When my father was dying I didn't have time to be angry at him. But I knew how much trouble he'd made—and you don't want to see that in your father. You want to turn him into a benevolent, innocent guy, and he wasn't. Didn't you ever argue with your father?"

I explain why not, citing a passage from Jonathan Franzen's novel *The Corrections*:

> She'd never really known her father. Probably
> nobody had. With his shyness and his formality . . .
> he protected his interior so ferociously that if you
> loved him, as she did, you learned that you could do
> him no greater kindness than to respect his privacy.

That's how it has always been with my father, I tell Lois. "If I want to be kind to him, I leave him in peace."

And Lois, that pit bull disguised as a wood nymph, writes back, "Weren't there times you were furious?"

Lois has a novelist's instinct, and wants to hear the conflict. So I tell her a story from years ago, from three or four years after my mother died. My initial grief over her death had settled down, but I was still frustrated that my father would never talk about her. Janir and I had gone east, and on Christmas Day I stood alone with Dad in his kitchen as he carved up a turkey. It was a bad time to say something, with everyone in the next room, but I couldn't stop myself. I'd been trying to get him to open up, to talk about the Christmas we spent in France when I was seven, about the tree with the burning candles clipped to the branches. I was angling, as usual, for some words about my mother. "Mom always loved that tree," I said.

"Yes, it was a French custom."

"Did she ever try to do one like that in Connecticut?"

"I think it would have been too great a fire hazard."

His answers were bland, they were impersonal and it pissed me off. I took a breath. "When was it that Mom first went off with other men?"

I knew he wouldn't tell me. I just wanted to rattle him, to drive him to some reaction—because I could feel how my mother was dying *right then*, every day he wouldn't talk about her. He kept carving the turkey. He had a ten-inch electric knife in his hand, and for a moment I imagined him plunging the blade into my chest. But of course he wasn't going to stab me. He wasn't going to respond at all. He went on slicing and laying out the pieces of turkey on an oval platter, not looking up, not saying anything.

We stood there for fifteen, maybe twenty seconds. I said, "I don't believe you didn't hear me."

He went on carving. "I heard you."

And that was the end of our talk, of our single argument. I was glad I'd challenged him, glad I'd spilled out what I knew. It didn't get me anywhere, but *that showed him*. Not once did I hear my parents argue, and I'm not very good at it myself.

Alzheimer's is ultimately a lethal disease, but most patients die first of some respiratory or cardiac failure. Dad has atrial fibrillation, asthma and other problems, but it's congestive heart failure that's likely to take him down. After three billion beats his heart is wearing out. It lacks the strength to pump blood up from his feet and ankles, and to clear the fluid from around his lungs. If all this were going on fifty years ago he'd be dead by now, but today the diagnostic tools are better, doctors know more, and the medications are more effective. Luckily, Dad has a supplemental health plan left over from his publishing days, with liberal drug benefits. He takes these medications every day:

- 5 mcg Coumadin, a blood thinner, to prevent clots
- 240 mg Cartia XT, to relax blood vessels and normalize heartbeat
- 125 mcg Digitek, to regulate heartbeat
- 40 mg Lasix, a diuretic
- 20 mEq Klor-Con, to prevent low potassium blood levels
- 4 mg Cardura, to treat prostate enlargement
- 10 mg lisinopril, an ACE inhibitor that relaxes blood vessels
- 150 mcg Levoxyl, to replace thyroid hormone
- 6 metered inhalations of Azmacort, for asthma
- 5 mg Aricept, to slow memory loss
- 20 mg Prozac, for depression

The number of pills often makes me wonder, but these are the medications that three or four physicians have agreed on. I give them to him. It's nothing I have to decide.

As the Alzheimer's patient loses, in a predictable and reverse order, the skills he acquired as a child—the ability to adjust the temperature of bath water, to use a toilet without assistance, to control his bladder, to control his bowels, to walk, to crawl—one loss is apt to worry the caretaker most. Bowel control.

I was cleaning the last of the windows, indoors, and Dad was in his bathroom off the kitchen, taking care of business. The odor was strong, but there was nothing unusual about that. I came and went, then peered in through the cracked door and found him standing in front of the toilet, facing out. Did he need some help?

He mumbled, and I opened the door.

He stood with his underwear around his knees. There was shit on the toilet seat, on the safety frame, on the bowl, and a considerable soft pile of it on the floor. His face had the furrowed, jerky look of dementia, and he held a roll of paper towels in his hand.

"*No,*" he said, when I reached for the towels. He waved me off, he didn't want me to come close. "I won't have you do it."

"I think you could use some help here."

"*No.*"

I fought a terrible urge to laugh. The shit was everywhere, it was a scene out of an asylum, and I was standing there trying to be polite with my father, trying to convince him to let me help. I turned a burst of laughter into a cough and made myself look serious. He was only going to spread the shit around more, so I took a towel, wet it at the kitchen sink, had him take hold of a grab bar with his right hand while I swabbed the left. I settled down and kept cleaning, but he resisted every move. He pulled back his hand, he didn't want me touching him. "This is my job," he said, but his resistance was fading. I got his socks and pants off, his underwear, his shirt and sweater, and started moving him toward the shower. I had to guide him the whole five feet. He looked dazed and shaky, a wrinkled, exhausted, shit-stained old man.

"Old age," I said. "It's ignominious, isn't it?"

"Yes, it is."

Though my dad never asks me anything about my life, past or present—not about my friends, not about the houses I've built or the novel I'm supposedly working on—he worries about me. When I climb a twenty-foot ladder to clean the upstairs windows from outside, he hobbles out of the house and along the gravel drive, far enough to where he can see me and make sure I'm okay. I sing down that I'm fine, but in fact the gusts of spring wind are making me nervous, and I'm glad he sticks around until I finish and descend.

Something wakes me at five in the morning. Perhaps it's the cries of the seagulls that gather on the baseball field on foggy mornings, thirty or forty of them strutting about and pecking at the grass, ignoring each other like junior high students at a dance. Or it might be that I picked up in my sleep how shallow my father's breathing has become, how he takes three breaths for every one of mine. I lie there listening to him over the monitor I've installed outside his room, thinking again about my parents' marriage.

Several times in my mother's last years, in varying states of depression and intoxication, she let me know that in their marriage it was my father who had first been unfaithful. I never really believed her, because that seemed so unlikely, so out of character for him. He was always quite proper, his eyes never followed some woman as she sauntered down a street or swayed across a beach. My eyes did, but Dad was endlessly respectful. Then, a couple of years ago, after I'd made an oblique reference to one of my mother's lovers, he brought up the topic of his infidelity.

"John," he said, "I don't want you to think badly of your mother, and there's something I should tell you. Before we were married I was involved with a girl from Virginia, and after I was married I went to see her. Just once, but I should not have done that. It hurt your mother and I've always been sorry for that. But you should know that I was the first to do something wrong, it was not your mother."

Immediately I wanted to know more about this woman. I asked Dad who she was and how he felt about her—but he had said his piece. He'd considered it unfair to stay silent about her any longer, but he was not going to give me any details.

I know a blast is coming when I tell Lois this story. To make it worse, I add a comment about how honorable my father was to make such a confession. After all, he didn't have to admit to being unfaithful, or to being the first. He could have kept all that hidden. Instead, he let me think worse about him so I wouldn't think worse about my mother. There's some honor to that, surely—but when I tell Lois, she howls.

"*Honorable?* No wonder your mother went out and screwed other men. Right at the start of the marriage he went off with somebody else? Do you know what that says to a woman? That she's not enough. That she's not pretty enough or smart enough or sexy enough. Your mother must have felt like killing him. *I* would have. He couldn't warm up to your mother, but he could run off with somebody else? A woman doesn't recover from that. Hey, you know I love your dad. He was always there for you. But there's an arrogance in him, in how he keeps his distance. You probably can't see it because you've got some of it in you, too."

Not all my friends are bent on rehabilitating me, but some of them—Sandy Weymouth, Kathy Galt, and especially Lois—like to needle me and uncover what I keep hidden, even from myself. I hate this, but need it. I don't like to think of myself as arrogant, but it's true that at times I close down to other people. After decades of trying to become the man my mother wouldn't leave, the transition is still incomplete. I'll talk, as my son puts it, about "broken hearts, emotions and feelings," but sometimes I shy away from people when their lives get too messy. Of course Lois can do the same. It's why she sees it so clearly in me.

May

Jane's daughter Susie has sent me some notes Dad left for her mother. They were written during their first years together, as Jane slept in—she seldom rose before ten—and my father left for work in the city. Until the day she died, Jane kept the notes on her bedside table.

Jane—

Please call when you are awake. I am in urgent need of advice on salad. Love, Joe

Darling—

I tried to switch off the alarm clock but don't know if I succeeded. We mustn't let the electrical devices get the better of us. Remember, we can always pull the plugs. Love, Joe

Darling—
If I fall off the Citadelle to join that pile of
bones below—it has been worth it for this
week. Have fun but buy to sell. Love, Joe

Darling—
I will be back about 6:45. How about taking in
the show at the laundromat. It is better than
some of the movies we have seen. Love, Joe

Darling—
It's spring! And the market is rising. And antiques
are doubling. Be of good cheer. Love, Joe

Dear Madame:
It was reported by our agent JJT that at 4 a.m.
June 13, 1979, your oil burner was in operation. This
is a clear violation of the President's guidelines.
You are henceforth forbidden to use, buy, sell,
produce, consume or profit in any way from the
production, consumption, or use of petroleum
products. James E. Schlesinger, Secretary of Energy

Darling—
Horoscope say this good day for you. As for me, I'll
be housecleaning all evening. Will call you. Love, Joe

Darling–

It's just as important to know when *not* to do something as to know when to do it. Think how much better off Philip II would have been if he had decided at the last moment not to send the Armada against England. Be of good cheer. I'll call you when I get home this afternoon. Love, Joe

Darling—

I love you—but don't tell your psychiatrist. Joe

Dearest Jane—

You have brightened my life more than I can tell you. May you always have as much joy as you have given me. With love, as always, Joe

Darling–

You are the most understanding of women. And I love you. Joe

Darling—

Lost in your bed: one pr. shorts. Love, Joe
P.S. This note not for general publication.

Simple, funny messages, each suggesting a story I'd like to hear. I have no evidence, on paper or otherwise, that my father was ever as playful as this with my mother. They were younger, perhaps the stakes were higher because of me and my brother, or perhaps it took Dad years to become this lighthearted. Or maybe Jane was simply a better match for him.

And I love you. I've never heard my father say that to any-one, ever.

I haven't longed to hear those words from him myself. I think it might dismay me now if he started telling me he loved me. I'd think some cog had busted in the old guy. What crushes me is the evidence that Lois is right, that he loved Jane but not my mother.

I want to believe in the romance of my parents' connection. Here I am in my dad's house, old enough to be a grandfather myself, searching back through my parents' history to find the spark between them. I don't want my father to have held him-self back, to have protected himself. I want him to have loved my mother, at least once upon a time.

Joe has arrived with Eliza, Dad's small and watchful granddaughter, and the minute Joe carries her into the room, Dad beams.

Though at first she keeps a somber distance from him, by the second day she's running freely around the living room and has created a little game that's technically between her and her father, but looks more like a way to get closer to my dad. She climbs down behind his lift chair and says, in a piping little voice, "I'm stuck!" She's two and a quarter and agile enough to scramble out on her own, but she likes her father to help. Once he lifts her out she flops down on the couch on her belly, then scrambles to her feet and peers around at my father in his chair. He responds with a look of shock and glee, at which she squeals and slithers back into her hideaway, and starts it all over again with a lilting, "I'm stuck!" They keep this up for twenty minutes.

It strikes me that Eliza is silly and blond and selfish and de-manding, and easily hurt and full of fun. Quite similar, indeed, to the last person who loosened my father up, his great and good

Joe Thorndike with his granddaughter Eliza, 2005

friend Jane. Perhaps my dad has come to such gleeful play with his granddaughter *because* he spent those years with Jane.

There's plenty of advice floating around about helpful things to do with an Alzheimer's patient:

> Reminisce about favorite times and/or hobbies. Take a box and fill it with photos and items that recall your loved one's favorite interests or former activities. He/she can take the items or photos out one at a time, and the two of you can share a story about it.

That's precisely what my father doesn't want to do. He doesn't want to soak himself in memories of Jane or my mother or his sons or anyone else. Even before his dementia he didn't want to do that. In the same pamphlet I read:

> Your touch can be a source of comfort. Hold your loved one's hand. Or gently massage

his/her hands, legs, and feet. A kiss or brush
of his/her hair may also be comforting.

Okay, the language is awkward. But the assumption is clear, that people want to be touched. Many do, I'm sure. I'd eat it up myself if someone would send in a home health aide for thirty minutes a day to massage my scalp. Then he/she could move on to my feet. But I can hardly imagine telling my father that someone is going to come in and give him a massage. "A *what?*"

Last winter my friend Elisabeth wrote that when her father was dying in France she embraced him in spite of his stiffness. "Even if my hugs were not shared, I'm happy I did it. I know his heart felt like doing it. I know also that his education didn't prepare him to relax, but all on the contrary, showed him how to stay 'cold' whatever happens."

Or here's Sue Miller, from her book about caring for her father: "In all this I tried to remember what I would want, dying. To feel loved, I thought. To feel connected to those I had loved. So I held him. I stroked his face, his hands. I kissed him."

Perhaps it would be easier for Dad if he had a daughter. But I'm the one he gets as old age overwhelms him. I have to put up with him, and he has to put up with me—and I don't think either of us is ready for me to start stroking his face.

In my four and a half months here I've seen one movie, gone to one dinner party, never spent a night away. I have a break coming in June, when Al will take over for me, and I don't want to get antsy now. But I am. I go out to play tennis, and once on the road I just want to keep going. I feel like I'm sixteen with a new license. My car is a little Nissan with 220,000 miles on it, but the thrill of rolling down the highway could not be greater if I were behind the wheel of a Pierce Arrow. It's the freedom of it, the miracle of sitting in a chair encased in a metal box and speeding over the surface of the earth. I could stay on the Mid-Cape Highway, cross the Sagamore Bridge and head straight to Denver to see Janir.

Dad wins everyone over. The podiatrist is glad to see him, and the women at the blood-work lab, and the hygienist who works on his teeth. He forgets their names but it doesn't matter. He creeps into the room on his walker, increasingly stooped and unsteady, and they all perk up. "You're back!" they say, and "How've you been?"

On good days and bad his answer is the same: "Getting along pretty well."

Jane once told me, "Everyone loves him. Everywhere we go, they all love him."

Dad, on the other hand, is less and less interested in other people. When a roofer comes over to present a bid, Dad goes into the bathroom and stays there until the guy leaves the property. When a chatty neighbor stops by with her two little dogs, he vanishes into his bedroom. He keeps as great a distance as he can from Jack Lane, who now comes twice a week.

Jack is a gentle, funny and sensitive guy. He stays out of Dad's way and could not be more respectful. He's a reader, a cook and a "thick Irishman," as he says. Dad can't stand him. "Every day he doesn't come is good for me." Also, "I just hold my breath when I go past him."

This may stem from Dad's worries about the bronchitis Jack reported when he first came to meet us. He was over it, but now Dad doesn't want to inhale any air that Jack has breathed. Going through the kitchen after Jack has been in there cooking, Dad holds his breath the whole way. It's awkward all around, but Jack is how I get to play tennis and I won't give him up. I explain this to my father, who nods in silence.

For my entire adult life my body and my father's have been the same. I slip easily into his coats, pants and shoes. Our collar size is the same, our sleeve length, and this spring I've been wearing his shirts. So when Dad steps into his morning shower, the body I see has to be my own corrupted body of the future: small frail chest, a butt that has all but vanished, underarm skin that wobbles. Sometimes when I step into the bathroom I find Dad staring at himself in the mirror. My presence never seems to inhibit him, and several times I've seen him duck his head or glance to one side, then snap back to his face as if trying to surprise himself.

"What do you see in there, Dad?"

"I don't know."

"Do you recognize yourself?"

"*No.*"

"Do you look older than you should?"

"It looks terrible."

It's common for elderly Alzheimer's patients to fail to recognize themselves, since the person they remember is so much younger than the decrepit soul staring back at them. My father, up close under the harsh light, looks truly worn out. His wizened skin is spotted with growths, and a yellowish discharge has crusted under his right eye. He's bent and twitchy, and I can imagine what a shock it must be for him to remember his sleek young self, and see this.

And if my father doesn't recognize himself, isn't it possible there are times he doesn't recognize me? Or Al or Joe or Harriet, or any of us? It's a common symptom of midstage Alzheimer's—though if it's happening, of course my father is covering it up. He'd never give himself away by asking who I am or what I'm doing here. But when he gets up in the morning and barely gives me a glance, he could be wondering who this guy is who seems to be living in his house. He doesn't stare at me as he does at himself in the mirror—but then, he wouldn't.

When my father is no longer polite, I'll know this disease has the better of him.

On the wall above my bed I've hung a photograph Dad took of my mother in 1950, standing in front of the snowy slopes of the upper Arlberg. She's thirty-four, slender and dark-haired, the mother of two. She holds her skis loosely over one shoulder and has wrapped her old-fashioned climbing skins—actual skins from a seal—around her waist. Even now, more

Virginia Thorndike in Lech, Austria, 1950

than half a century later, I can still be lifted up by this glimpse of my mother: the strength in her limbs, her confident pose, her luck and grace. Those were the best of times for my parents, yet only fifteen years later my mother would be divorced, lonely and overweight. And ten years after that she'd be dead.

It's on these mornings, when I swim up out of sleep and dreams to find her gazing down on me from the wall, so much younger than I am now, that I miss her most. Over the years she's the one I've wept for.

After dinner I announce, "Here are tonight's three choices. We can watch the last installment of *Victory at Sea*, we can read from *The Wind in the Willows*, or we can do nothing and have a house full of peace and quiet."

"I think peace and quiet."

After an entire day spent dozing in his chair, all Dad wants after dinner is more of the same.

Undeterred, I make a trip the next day to the children's room at the library. I've noticed in recent weeks that Dad has been drifting off to Horatio Hornblower and Toad of Toad Hall, and I suspect that those stories have become too complex for him to follow. So now I bring home the first of the Babar books by Jean de Brunhoff. Babar seems just right: the prose and drawings are simple, and once upon a time it was Dad who read this book to me. The series has been attacked for its colonialist views, but I'm liberated from such cavils—along with so much else—because all I care about is making my father happy. The book starts with tragedy, it's true, as Babar's mother is shot by a hunter. But the story soon turns whimsical, as the young elephant is taken in by an old woman in Paris, who outfits him in new clothes and spats. Dad pays attention, as far as I can tell, all the way through. We finish the book in a single sitting, and tomorrow I'll read him another. The library is full of them.

On a rainy Saturday with the kind of schedule Dad prefers—nowhere to go and no one coming over—I decide not to start any conversations or to ask him any questions. I want to see how much he'll say if not goaded into it. I keep a pad close by and write down all the words he speaks. The first sentence comes at 8:25 in the morning.

Do you think you could get me a couple of glasses of water?

This is followed, during the day, by *Oh, thank you.*

Shall I go back in there?

Didn't I just take a shower?

Let me get by here.

Oh, good.

And finally, over dinner, *Do we have any obligations today?*

We don't. But as I point out, it's almost eight at night.

Do we have any obligations tomorrow?

Nothing tomorrow, I tell him, though Harriet is coming so I can play tennis.

Okay, that might be it for the day: forty-seven words. But then, after another long quiet spell, he asks, *Do you know if the prong sticking out of the house is still there?*

I smile wildly. My dad, who can't remember the names of the most common household objects, has somehow come up with that gorgeous word *prong*. I ask all kinds of questions to figure out what he's talking about, but whatever it is, he can't explain it.

The prong sticking out of the house. I go around for days, repeating the phrase to myself.

After looking through papers from my father's college years, I read to him from some old copies of the *Crimson,* and from a paper he wrote for an economics class. No response to any of that, but then he asks, "Did I tell you about Harvard?"

"No, what?"

"Where we got a . . . uh . . . we got . . . a dog. We put . . . how did we do this? We put . . . what was it?"

Long pauses. I sense that he remembers the story but can't get at the words, so I wait, and eventually he finds the thread. "It was something agreeable to eat. We put it on the steps of the *Crimson*."

Ah. I've heard this story before. "You found a bulldog," I say.

"Yes! That was it. A bulldog. We got a picture of him licking the steps of the *Crimson*."

"You put a Yale sweater on him."

"That's right."

"It was before a football game," I remind him. "I think you smeared some hamburger or something on the statue of John Harvard."

"Not hamburger. It was . . . " He can't bring it back.

"Something to make the Yale bulldog lick John Harvard's feet."

"That was it."

"Did you print that picture?"

"You bet."

We're both happy to have rescued this wonderful prank. And hoping to keep Dad engaged after that burst of conversation, I open another folder, this one from his high school years. There are notebooks from his Latin classes, a somber graduation photo and his valedictory address. Also, oddly, a studio portrait of a pleasant but somewhat homely girl. I show it to my dad, but he doesn't remember who it is. On the back is her name. "Shirley Brock," I say.

"Oh yes." He takes the photo and stares at it for a moment before handing it back. "Yes, I remember her. I admired her."

"For what?"

"Well, she . . . she . . . I knew her." He doesn't look awkward or embarrassed, but he struggles with his words. "She entertained boys in her room."

"Did she really? What kind of entertaining was that?"

"I'd say it was . . . " A long pause, which I do nothing to interrupt. His tone is unchanged: "It was a little mutual cocksucking, I would say."

I clamp down hard to keep from laughing, and to stay on my chair. I don't want to spook him, because I want to hear more. That *word!* Dad seems unaware that he has said anything out of the ordinary, though in all our years together I've never heard anything like it.

"It doesn't mean I did that. You see, I had to walk over to the trolley car in those days. It was a long ride to New York."

"Was her room near the trolley?" And when he doesn't answer, "Did you know people who'd been over to her room?"

"Oh yes."

"Were there a lot of them?"

"Quite a number. But my father knew all about her. It wouldn't have done."

He delivers this as neutrally as everything else he's said, and that's the end of it, I can't get any more out of him. But long after he settles into silence a smile keeps erupting on my face. Of course I'll be reporting this to Al, and to Janir, and every time I think about it a laugh starts boiling up.

Whenever I mention to someone that my father has Alzheimer's, I hear another story.

Danny, who's shingling the roof, tells me that he and his wife looked after her father for a year. The old man carried a piece of paper in his pocket and showed it to Danny over and over, sometimes every five minutes. It said, "I'm brain dead."

A guy I play tennis with tells me about his father-in-law, an erstwhile respectful guy who started yelling and throwing things and grabbing at every female nurse who came close.

Ralph, who runs my water department back in Ohio, tells me on the phone that he and his siblings spent years looking after his mother. Toward the end she was frail but had one desire, to get out of the house. At night they put her in a hospital bed with railings, but she climbed over them. Later, when she could no longer get over them, she tried to squeeze through them, and Ralph would find her wedged half in and half out of the bed. He moved downstairs and slept in her room, but all night she talked and cried out to him. She was wide awake, having slept all day. Occasionally she escaped from the house and the neighbors would call. Six years this went on, until she died.

Of course I hear more stories these days because I'm on the lookout for them. But the statistics back up my impressions. Half of everyone over eighty-five now has Alzheimer's, and as the average age of the population rises, so will the prevalence of the disease. It may lie within us for decades, hardly progressing, perhaps waiting for the body to slow down—no one knows for sure. Everyone is fighting to stay healthy and live longer, but the better we keep our bodies in shape the more likely we'll be to end our days with some kind of dementia. It's enough to turn one into a gourmand and a wastrel.

No matter what filters I try to see Dad's troubles through—the books I read about Alzheimer's, the people I talk to, the pair of workshops I've attended—it grinds me down when he spends an entire day in his chair and says nothing, then another day and another.

I try to keep some perspective. Only a week ago we had that great night when he told me about the bulldog licking John Harvard's feet, and the mutual cocksucking girl in high school. But since then he's been in such a funk that I wonder if he'll ever enjoy himself again. At what point will he be so unhappy, and his pleasures so few—and my own patience so thin—that I'll hope for him to die?

With help from Al, Dad has all his medical directives in place. His Living Will reads in part, "If my suffering is intense and irreversible, I do not want to have my life prolonged. I would then ask not to be subjected to surgery or resuscitation. I would wish in such cases to have no life support from mechanical ventilators, intensive care services, or other life-prolonging procedures."

This is standard legal language that Al used to address the heroic measures Dad wished to avoid: resuscitation with its frequent broken ribs, and the intubation required with a ventilator. They were thinking in a traditional way, imagining an irreversible suffering that stemmed from some breakdown of Dad's body, or else the persistent vegetative state he wanted no part of. But late-stage Alzheimer's, even in someone as old as my father, can make an end run around medical directives. It could leave Dad fully conscious and in passable health, but anguished and completely isolated. If he reaches that stage we'll still be working to keep him alive, but we won't know if that's what he wants, and neither will he. I'm sure we'll just wait it out, hoping that nature will take its course—as the doctors say when they're ready to let a patient die.

In fact, we're pretty far from nature around here already. If we took Dad off his potent medications, I think we'd see nature take its course pretty quick, and I'm not ready for that.

After assuming for months that my father's old films are irrecoverable, I go on eBay and for ten bucks find an 8 mm projector that works perfectly. I test it out with the abandoned reel of my mother's slow-motion dives, then sit Dad down after dinner three nights in a row to watch some of the dozens of hours of film he took when Al and I were young, mostly of us swimming and diving, riding bikes, throwing rocks, waterskiing and playing Ping-Pong, our endless life of games. Boring to anyone else!

Dad seems somewhat responsive, and each night I sit him closer to the flickering rectangle on the wall. To help him out I name most of the people who appear: Whitney and Tony Goit, Nick and Grant Monsarrat, my cousins Barbie and Mike and Mona.

He seems to remember them, but I can't be sure. Tony Goit, certainly. He was my brother's best friend and shows up often in the films, a boy with a flair to everything he did. There's a long sequence of Al and Tony as teenagers, playing a kind of soccer on the street as they wheel about on a pair of Solexes, the tiny French motorbike. They are beautiful boys, perhaps fifteen, and the camera lingers on them. Tony smiles and laughs: he always had the most expressive face.

They both went to Dartmouth. After graduation Al went into the Coast Guard, and Tony taught school. He was good at teaching, I think, but slid into emotional turmoil and drug use. After a long troubled period he shot himself.

There's a letter in my father's files from Tony's dad, Charlie, written shortly after my mother died.

> Dear Joe,
>
> I am so sorry to hear of Virginia's death. My most vivid memories of her were at the Roman Banquet you two had so many years ago. Then it seemed that life would go on forever with modest ups and downs perhaps, but rich withal. Where is the peace and serenity we were promised for these autumn years?
>
> Poor Virginia, she had less than the rest of us, and ours is a meager pittance.
>
> Perhaps your sons will come to be closer to you. I think you need that badly, Joe. There is really very little to cling to. I know—half my life went with Tony.

What courage he had to write that to my father: *you need that badly, Joe.* Though Charlie died some years ago, I love him now for making that try.

In my insistent evangelical way I want to make Dad watch more of these films every night. I want to clobber him with Tony Goit in his last days of pure youth. I want to find the images of my smiling mother and show them forward and back, over and over. If I compiled her appearances on a single reel I could tie Dad to his chair and make him watch until he broke down and started to talk. How long would it take?

Perhaps the fleeting glimpses of my mother and Tony and my cousin Mona—all suicides—are already too painful for him. He could be sitting there with his face a mask but thinking about his own youth, about our beautiful but doomed family, about Margery, about Jane. I hope for all that. I'm still trying to effect his last-minute conversion into a guy who will let some emotion out.

I fold up the machine and let him rest. But tomorrow I'll set it up again, because Al and Ellen will be here.

After putting Dad to bed I go upstairs and dig out Charlie Goit's letter and lie down with it. I know about that Roman Banquet, at which six couples, dressed in togas, ate chicken my mother baked in clay. I hold Charlie's letter in my hand—*half my life went with Tony*—and finally I begin to cry, sobbing hard with my face in a pillow. I'm crying for my mother and for Tony, and for my confused father, and for Al who can't stand to think of our mother, and for myself as I cling to our past.

Al came down to the Cape for ten days, and I drove out to Ohio to look after my rentals. I repaired screens, opened bathroom drains, rehung doors, signed leases, and mowed waist-high grass. There was too much work, but it was lovely not to be taking care of anyone. Every intoxicating hour was my own, the sun beat down, and sometimes I just wandered around on my farm in a daze. I lay down in the waving spring grass and let the clouds pass by.

On my last night Billy Renz threw a party at my house. Billy and I have put on a dozen Spring Dances over the years, and this time, because I had so much going on, he did all the work himself: sent out the invitations, put three hundred songs on his computer, jacked up the sound system and moved most of the furniture out of the one large room in my house. We had the usual potluck with young and old, badminton, croquet, and an egg toss out in the meadow. At dusk the dancing began, as it always has, with the Isley Brothers' *Who's That Lady?* and by midnight

June

we were all on our backs with our bare feet in the air, wriggling and hooting and rolling over each other in the alligator dance. We've been going crazy like this in Athens for thirty years.

Best of all, as the party wound down, I lay on my bed in a corner of the room with Kathy, Michelle, Didi, and Billy. Among the five of us we have two hundred years of friendship. I'd come back to Ohio because of my rentals, but what I really needed was to be held, to laugh and tell stories, and to know I still fit into my old life.

Over the last few months I've developed the common caregiver's illusion that only I can look after my father. But while I was gone Al stepped in and took care of everything. Things went so smoothly that when I checked in from Ohio I was disappointed. I wanted him to find it more difficult, to be overwhelmed, to be stunned by what I go through every day.

In my reports to Al, all winter and spring, I've subtly played up everything that has gone awry. How satisfying it is to describe how the heat went out during the blizzard, or how we had to go to the hospital and were kept there for nine hours, or how Dad crapped on the floor again. All this proves I'm indispensable and earning my keep.

When Al and Joe are most appreciative, or when someone praises me for moving in with my father, I shrug off their comments and act like it's no big deal. But underneath I soak up the approval. "Anything can be endured if all humanity is watching," writes the novelist James Salter. "We live in the attention of others."

On one of my Athens nights I had dinner with my old friend Beth Kaufman, whose father's dementia is more advanced than my dad's. He lives with his wife of fifty years, but no longer recognizes her. He thinks she's a woman who comes in to cook his meals. Recently, after a dinner he enjoyed, he asked her, "Do you accept tips?"

Beth and I could laugh at this story with its underlying heartache: at some point what can you do but laugh? But when I returned to my dad's I wondered again if he sometimes forgets who I am. There's a cocked, watchful look he gives me when I wake him in the morning, and his responses to me, when I set out his medications or bring him a meal, can seem polite and formulaic. He could be speaking to an aide he barely knows.

And now some cord has been broken, or frayed at least, between me and my father. When I talk to him he nods, sometimes smiles, is polite about all things but has nothing to say. He doesn't want to leave the house, doesn't want to sit in the remodeled sunroom, doesn't perk up at anything. Perhaps the fact that I left has undermined his trust. Or maybe he's just seeing through me. Because while outwardly I'm still gentle and cheerful, his decrepit state can make me squirm. It gets to me when he lies in his chair with his head back and his mouth gaping like a dead man's. He suffers from sleep apnea, in which the soft tissues in his throat close down, his breathing stops and he wakes with a honk, several times a minute. He's unaware of what's happening, and of course it's no fault of his own—yet some piece of me hates him for it. When he's weakest, when he's stubborn and failing, I have flashes of repugnance. He comes out of the bathroom hunched over his walker, his face gaunt and hair disheveled. He's now religious about holding his breath as he passes through the kitchen—because not just Jack, but other people have breathed in there. At first this seemed amusing, an "endearing quirk," as Al puts it. But this morning, when Dad reached the living room and gave a little puff of exhalation, as if he'd completed a dangerous passage, I thought, *You pitiful old man.*

We sit at the table for dinner, Dad with a bowl of the haddock stew Jack has cooked. I finish my own meal in a couple of minutes. I've started a juice diet—one of my tenants in Ohio was thirty days into a diet of only juices, and he looked both thin and buoyant—and after two glasses I'm done. Dad eats so slowly I can't watch. His spoon rattles against his bowl, then against his teeth. I think I should reach out to him in some way, find something we can talk about. Instead I pick up a magazine and read an article. For thirty minutes I disappear. Later, holding the Azmacort inhaler to his mouth—always an intimate act—I sense the distance between us. I'm awkward as I bring the inhaler close, and there's a faint hesitation as he puts his lips to it.

At night, alone in my room upstairs, I pull the notes my father wrote to Jane out of their manila envelope. Darling——. Dearest Jane——. You have brightened my life more than I can tell you. You are the most understanding of women. And I love you.

I'm glad my father had three good decades with Jane. I'm glad that love came to him at the end of his life. But Lois asks, "Do you think if he treated your mother the way he did Jane, that she'd have stayed? That she'd still be alive and you'd still have her?"

I lie in my room, with the notes spread out on the bed, and wonder about it. Maybe she'd have wandered anyway—but maybe not, if my father had been more affectionate and playful. Instead, he kept his distance. He folded his arms, he sat upright on the couch or leaned faintly away from her, he never reached over and took a bit of food off her plate. At night he slept in his single bed. I never heard him tell my mother how good she looked or smelled or felt. Maybe late in the evening, when Alan and I were asleep, he was telling her she was the most understanding of women, or the prettiest, or smart and inventive. Maybe he did tell her he loved her. I just don't have any evidence of that.

Years ago I chose the parent I would save from the burning house. Now I wind up tied to my other parent, my father, the one I've struggled not to be like. Yet the rage Lois suggests I should feel about my father doesn't come to me. Instead, over the last six months I've grown closer to him. I don't know if he feels close to me or not. There aren't many signs that he does. I have those flashes of aversion, but I take them to be signs of fear, not anger or deception. It's brutal to watch your father slide into oblivion—and to imagine your own decline to come—but day after day I still want to be here in his house. I lay my hands on him, I listen to everything he says, and every morning I'm glad to see his face.

Leafing through a book from Dad's shelves, I find a chapter called "Henry Luce Starts a Picture Magazine," with selections from the diaries of *Life*'s first managing editor, John Shaw Billings. I read some passages to Dad, and this finally gets him talking. When Billings mentions the layout rooms—where the two-page spreads of text and pictures were pinned to the walls, to be adjusted and refined as each issue took shape—Dad tells me his office was right next door to those rooms. "That way I got my word in on anything that came up."

"Did you have to maneuver for that office?"

"I did."

"So is it true what they say, that you were both mulish and ambitious?"

Dad laughs. "I guess I was."

"And were others resentful that you snagged that office?"

"Oh yes."

"Like who?"

"Longwell, for one. I was supposed to be working directly for him, you see. I wasn't, I was working for Billings."

"But Longwell was your boss for three years."

"Yes, but I didn't recognize him as such."

This comes with a grin. It's clear that *Life* was always crowded, as my father once wrote, with "plenty of cooks standing around ready to get in the broth." And Luce, as he noted, tended to play off his subordinates against one another.

W. A. Swanberg, in his book *Luce and His Empire*, confirms Henry Luce's habit of pitting his editors against each other to get more out of them. "Blood was flowing," he writes. "Promotions of importance were made not only on the basis of past good work, but also after a couple of candidates had fought for the job. Since they knew they were fighting for the job, a kind of jungle savagery sometimes resulted."

It's hard for me to imagine my father sharpening his knives, but the fact is that he followed Billings and Longwell into the job of managing editor. Once there, Dad's style was to rule with a loose hand. He allowed his subordinates, especially Edward Thompson, who became the fourth ME, to run their departments with little interference—which left Dad free to follow some broader, more intellectual interests. As Loudon Wainwright notes in *The Great American Magazine*, "He was the instigator of a number of substantial articles on contemporary American life (on art, atomic energy and the national character) and was responsible for the first major series *Life* ever ran, ten long, illustrated articles on the history of Western Man."

These articles evolved into a book that did well for *Life*, selling half a million copies. On Dad's shelves there's a morocco-clad edition, which I pull down and open on the dining room table in front of him. Dad glances at it, but by now, after his brief flurry of conversation, he's already sinking. Leaning over his shoulder, trying to keep his attention, I read to him the caption to a two-page illustration of a fresco from the Sistine Chapel, a sentence likely written by my father himself: "The golden sheaves of artistic genius, ripening for three centuries in sunny Italy, were gathered at last into one man: Michelangelo Buonarroti."

Surprising me, Dad reaches out and closes the book, almost slams it shut, and pushes it away. He's had enough talk, it seems.

Enough of Michelangelo, and perhaps enough of me. After his petulant gesture, I've had enough of him. For several minutes we sit at the table, looking down, neither of us speaking or moving. Then the slow rhythm of his bedtime rolls over us, soothing us both. I throw his clothes in the laundry, I set out what he'll need for tomorrow, I sit on the chair by his bed. It's daily life. He's like an undemanding child, and the work calms me.

Dad has finally run Jack off. For me Jack was perfect— easy to get along with, funny, and a great cook. But Dad hated him from the start and told him, the last time he was here, to stay out in the sunroom once he finished cooking. So Jack talked to me. "I can take it," he said, "it doesn't offend me. But here's your dad toward the end of his life and he's putting up with someone he hates. He shouldn't have to do that, so I don't think I should continue."

I'll have to look for someone else, because I don't want to give up tennis. Dad won't like someone new coming in, but he'll have to live with it. *Damn him*, anyway. Right now I don't care about everything he's done for me my whole life. I've given up plenty to move to his house, and he can't put up with the easygoing Jack Lane for six hours a week?

I'm cold and efficient as I serve him dinner. This is covert, I know, but I have no history of working things out with my father, of discussing our differences, of engaging in an outright argument. I suppose I could explain how much trouble he's making for me, and so get it off my chest. But I don't. I act, in short, pretty much as he would, and just tell him I'm going to find someone else. He might not like the new person, but twice a week I am going to play tennis. I'm calm, but beat him up with the obvious, that he's making it hard on me. He nods and looks away. He doesn't retreat, and neither do I.

Dad can still read, but doesn't. Not books, and rarely a magazine. Tonight as I cook dinner he spends fifteen minutes poring over the latest *New Yorker*. I watch him as he moves through it backward, examining page after page of text and photos. He goes so slowly and seems so completely absorbed that I'm sure he must be reading something, if only the ads. But when I come in with his plate and set it on the table, I find he's looking at the magazine upside down.

It makes me wonder about all those home movies I've subjected him to. If it doesn't matter to him if a still photograph is right side up or not, what can he make of my mother diving off a high board, or Alan and Tony playing soccer on motorbikes? To him it could be all just flickering lights.

After dinner the two of us sit in the living room as I read in silence a twenty-page family history that Dad wrote at my urging years ago. "All my ancestors," it begins, "so far as I know, lived on the North Shore of Massachusetts, from the time when the first of them arrived on this continent."

He explains how the original John Thorndike came over from England in 1630, possibly with Governor Winthrop on the *Arbella*. He raised seven children here but returned to England as an old man and was buried in Westminster Abbey. His stone there, my father notes wryly, is now covered up by a souvenir stand.

Dad tells the story of his ancestor George Jacobs, who was hanged in Salem as a wizard.

He tells quirky stories of Thorndikes, Buxtons and Farnhams, stories heard when he was a child. There was my grandmother's Aunt Mehitabel, who was snatched from her cradle by a bear and carried off into the woods, then rescued by her brothers—surely an apocryphal tale. There was an uncle who took off for the California gold rush, leaving a wife and children who never heard from him again. There was Aunt Lizzie, who married a

French baker, a union looked down upon by the rest of the family. "If you look through the family album of daguerreotypes," my father writes, "you will see that all the other sitters appear in formal, dignified portraits. But François Renou was photographed, most cruelly, at full length, in all his dropsical girth."

My father's parents married as the century turned, in 1900.

> Though they were never well off, they always
> had a maid in the house, and one of the first
> automobiles in town, and one of the first telephones
> (Peabody 79). They were founding members of
> the country club and the women's club and my
> father was a director of all three local banks.
> In the summer they sometimes rented a cottage
> on the shore at Marblehead with friends or went
> to a friend's camp in New Hampshire. These
> were much the same places and times and people
> seen in Winslow Homer's paintings of the Maine
> Coast and the White Mountains. It was also the
> time of the Gibson girl, as can be seen in the
> pictures of my mother leaning over my cradle.

Dad goes on in his family history to describe his college years and his move to New York. He writes about his wedding to my mother, tells stories about our stay in Europe, and closes the history with this passage about the day we returned from France to our house on Owenoke Road:

> We were all glad to get back to Westport in the
> spring of 1950. The Goit boys and the Monsarrat
> boys were waiting and so was Debbie Bradley—she
> and Alan having borne their separation bravely.
> Our place, then and for the years to come, was
> Owenoke. John and Alan do not need my help in

recalling those years. For John the sun of memory
had already risen and for Alan it was just coming up.

Reading that phrase, *the sun of memory*, I break into silent tears.
I sit on my chair in the living room and cry but hold it in, glanc-
ing across the room at my father's bony and exhausted face. I
can't look at him. Memory, for my dad, is a kind of sunlight that
plays across our lives. It makes history possible. He was glad to
see the onset of memory in his young boys—but it's devastating now to watch that sun as it sets in him.

Just as I'm getting up in the morning I hear a sharp
little cry and a thump over the monitor, and run downstairs to
find Dad on the floor beside his bed. He doesn't look hurt, so
I settle down with him and hold his hand and ask him if he's
in pain anywhere. No no, he's fine, he's perfectly okay. Except
he can't get up. After ten minutes I pull his arms toward me
and raise his torso to a sitting position, but he can't maintain
it on his own. I maneuver behind him, slip my arms under his
and dead-lift him onto the bed. Onto me, actually, as I collapse
back onto the mattress. He's completely rigid, but for the first
time I have my father in my arms. I rest for a moment, then
wriggle out from under him, and as soon as I get him stretched
out head-to-foot on the bed he goes to sleep.

I don't know what I'd do if he fell out in the living room,
away from his bed. Drag him into his bedroom, I guess, because
I could never stand him up on my own. It makes me consider
one of the advantages of a nursing home: that in an emergency
there are always plenty of attendants around. But later in the day,
when I call Dotty Turner to ask how Oliver's doing, she tells me
she's unhappier than ever about his care. Recently she went in at
eleven in the morning and found him lying in his own diarrhea.
She chased down an attendant but was told Oliver would have

to wait, everyone was busy. The smell was overwhelming. She complained at the nurses' station and finally got some reluctant help. But how often did this happen when she wasn't there? She only goes in for an hour or two a day.

"These places are all short-handed," she tells me. "They don't want to move Oliver into his wheelchair, it's too much work. They never take him outside. They might do something for him right now, but they won't do it regularly. They're all too busy. I got them to brush his teeth a few times, but then they stopped. Everyone's in a hurry. The feeding room is the worst, I hate to go in there. They purée the food and spoon it in too fast. There's always somebody coughing or choking."

Her bottom line: "I pray to God I won't have to go into one of those places."

And: "If you can possibly stay with your dad, do it."

Then, only twelve hours after our talk, Oliver dies in his sleep. And now I don't know if I should tell my father.

I've waited a day. I've talked to my brothers and my son, to Harriet and Dotty and Lois and Sandy. Some think Dad should be told, others think there's no reason for him to know. But I feel I have to tell him. I wouldn't want him to suggest, some weeks from now, that we call Oliver on the phone or go down for a visit. While the news will be a blow, I can't start deciding which emotions my father is allowed to have.

July

All his life my father has read and studied. He loved the nuances of diction and grammar, and was devoted to words the way some men are devoted to sports. He would watch an occasional movie, but until he was seventy I never saw him sit down in front of a television. He watched standing up, as if at any moment he might have to leave the room. He preferred the written word, loved a good letter and wrote thousands of them.

I'm still going through his papers, and yesterday found another cardboard box filled with letters. There could be a thousand in this box alone, half of them sent to my father from other people, the rest carbons of the letters he mailed out. This batch covers about five years, and includes neither family letters nor memos from work, all of which are in other boxes. Here old friends write from the ranch they've moved to in Colorado, or from their home by Lake Champlain. They write him from Tokyo or London or Bronxville, New York. People write to ask for a job at *Heritage*, or to congratulate him about his latest book, or to ask if he can help get *their* book published. Letters of recommendation go out for a dozen sons and daughters of friends. A neighbor, Ina Bradley, writes that our young and rambunctious Gordon setter, Homer, has trampled their flower gardens and left excrement on their flagstones. Clipped to her letter is Dad's reply, in which he promises to do everything "humanly and caninely possible" to curtail Homer's depredations. He affirms, on a long typed page, that "dogs must be able to leave the house, and it lies in the inherent nature of dogs to roam," but that he will "initiate a study of Homer's routines, in the hope of finding a way to alleviate this problem." He is respectful, considerate and neighborly—but there is a whiff of the bottom line, that Ina might as well buck up, because nothing can be done short of leashing the dog, and that's not going to happen.

Trained as a journalist, my father wrote swiftly and well. For seventy-five years the pages poured out of his typewriter. Yet now he can't address an envelope or leave me the simplest note. I think one reason he doesn't answer the phone anymore is that he can't take a message.

We expect people to fail in old age, but in a year this disease has reduced my father to the bones of language. In writing, he's finished. In speech, he might still have a thousand nouns—but they don't always come when he wants them. How he struggles when a word escapes him. He sits in his chair, his hand rises to his face. There's something he wants to name but he can't pull it out.

"They're . . . they're rolled up," he says. "They're . . . "

I play a kind of twenty questions with him. Are they something you eat? Can you wear them? Are they soft? Are they made of paper? Is it paper towels? When we can't get it, his face scrunches up and he shudders. It looks like a wave of pain going through his body.

Everything I do in this house is to keep my father well. At the same time, I quail before the idea that he could rebound into solid physical health. What keeps me sane is that his body's decline has matched his mind's. My hope is to stay with him until he dies, right here in his house—but what, Al asks, if he goes on for another year, for two or three more years?

No no, he has to die so I can have my life back.

The past couple of weeks he has hobbled along neither better nor worse. I think it's this that's getting under my skin, that leads me to go to bed early and lie on my back with the light on but nothing to read. Out of all the books in this house, there's not one that interests me. This is not a good sign, but I don't tell my brothers. When they call I tell them I'm fine. I don't say I was disappointed when Dad chose not to go to Oliver's service. Everyone else was relieved, and I pretended to feel the same— but in fact I wanted to take a drive, to get out of the state, to put Dad to the test. I wanted to see how hard it would be for him to face Oliver's casket. I wanted to bring him back slumped in his seat and unable to walk into the house. I wanted some action, some trouble, some reason for me to be here.

My father once wrote an article for *American Heritage* about our ancestor George Jacobs, who was hanged in Salem during the witchcraft trials. I read it again this afternoon: "My Ancestor the Wizard."

Jacobs was about eighty years old, with long white hair and no teeth. He fit the pattern of those accused by the young girls who initiated the hysteria. "He walked with two staffs," my father wrote. "He was short-tempered and irascible." The investigating magistrates looked for the mark of the Devil on him—a third teat—and believed they found it. Even more damaging was the lack of daily prayer in his house, as reported by his servant girl.

"Let us then hear you say the Lord's Prayer," commanded one of the magistrates. This was considered a crucial test, for it was believed that someone possessed by the Devil could not recite this prayer. Jacobs faltered. He began to speak, he stopped, he tried again and went silent. Like any Puritan in Salem he'd grown up with the Lord's Prayer, quite possibly had said it daily—yet now he could not retrieve it.

"It should be remembered," my father wrote, "that he was very old. He was under stress. He may have had the lapses of memory that many old people have. Or he may not have been much of a praying man. But to the magistrates, his failure to complete the Lord's Prayer was probably the most damning evidence of all."

In August of 1692 George Jacobs was hanged on Salem's Gallows Hill, under the eye of a man dressed all in black who'd come down from Boston on horseback to assure that the hangings went as planned: the zealot Cotton Mather.

Reading between the lines, it seems quite possible that Jacobs was not just an irascible old man, but one who suffered from some kind of dementia, and that his loss of memory led directly to his death.

Over dinner I asked my dad if he could recite the Lord's Prayer. "I think so," he said, and ran smoothly through the first third, as far as, "on earth as it is in heaven." But there he stopped. He couldn't make the jump to "Give us this day our daily bread" and the lines that follow. Of course, he's not much of a praying man. I teased him a little, saying that in seventeenth-century Salem his forgetfulness could have placed him in jeopardy.

This was a mistake. After a few more bites of dinner he set down his spoon. His eyes closed, his face fell apart and he had nothing more to say. Later we listened to Garrison Keillor, but there were no easy laughs from Dad, and as soon as the show was over he went into his room and lay down for the night. I sat in the dining room and berated myself. How can I have been so stupid?

Often we sit quietly at dinner, saying nothing, but tonight Dad seems more alert than usual, which leads me to read him a book he's been saving for his granddaughter, Beatrix Potter's *The Tale of Peter Rabbit*. Though over a hundred years old, the story could have been written yesterday. It was read to me when I was young, and Dad tells me his mother read it to him when *he* was young.

After Peter Rabbit, I read him some passages from his own "Family History." I love this one, in particular:

> Between my parents' marriage and the birth of their only child, thirteen years elapsed. That period, extending roughly from the turn of the century to the eve of World War One, was an uncommonly happy time for those who were established in the main stream of American life. When I read the marvelous opening paragraph of Gibbon's *Decline and Fall of the Roman Empire*, I feel that I could almost be reading a description of the Edwardian era in the United States. Gibbon's phrases describe the age of the Antonines but they could apply almost as well to the decade before I was born.

That leads me to Gibbon himself, and from Dad's copy I read out loud the first paragraph, then several more pages. He seems completely attentive throughout: he corrects my pronunciation of Queen Boadicca (Bo-ADD-uh-kuh) and explains that both she and Caractacus, another Celtic leader, gave fierce resistance to the emperor Claudius's invasion of Britain in the first century AD. It's a roller-coaster ride around here, but an evening like this, when his memory seems to be working, pours over me like balm.

Jane died a year ago today. I've thought about it all day long but haven't mentioned her name.

After two days in which Dad leaves his bed only for meals, this morning after breakfast he starts moving around the house. With new strength comes new mania. He must find "the larger push pins" to anchor some photos to the wall. There have never been any larger push pins, but he is sure they are here somewhere. I leave him staring at the desk, and come back after mudding the drywall ceiling in the sunroom to find him standing over fifty of the regular pins that he has dropped on the floor. He's trying, ponderously, to brush them together using a shirt draped from his hand. I pick them up for him, against his wishes, and once the job is done he starts to wander off without his walker. He hasn't moved five feet without his walker in a month.

I go back to my drywall, and when I come back he's in the bathroom, perhaps shaving. I don't go barging in, but after a long quiet spell I have a look. His pants are off and he's dipping his Depends in the sink full of water. They don't look or smell bad, but he clutches them and won't let me take them. Calming words, a slow persistence on my part, and slowly I bring him around to the known routine of dressing.

Two stories about my dad from when I was a child.

We were driving back from Rome to Antibes in the south of France, in the tiny Renault station wagon my parents bought for our European stay. With our housekeeper, Nana, there were five of us, so our luggage rode on the roof rack, wrapped in a tarpaulin. We stopped for lunch at some *trattoria* and waited for the meal. Thieves had been a problem, and after twenty minutes Dad went out to check on the car. Sure enough, he found the tarp on the ground and two men lifting down the bags.

"*Hey!*"

They dropped the bags and took off. Dad pursued them, running down into the cobbled streets of town. They were young, he was young, it was a real race. His sport jacket flapped, the streets grew narrower, finally he pulled up.

We were all standing by the car when he got back, still breathing hard. He explained what happened and said, still surprised at himself, "What would I have done if I had caught them?"

I was only seven and don't actually remember any of this— but it's how my mother and Nana used to describe it.

Then the story of Earl Graves, the younger brother of Nana's husband. Earl had killed a man in Virginia. He'd had an argument in a bar, gone back to his house, taken a knife from his kitchen, returned to the bar and stabbed the guy. His sentence was relatively light for premeditated murder—perhaps, as my father once pointed out to me, because it was one black man killing another. In 1952, after eight years in prison, he was released with no job and nowhere to live.

Dad told Nana he could stay with us.

He was the gentlest of men, this murderer, or so it seemed to me. Not that I knew at the time what he'd done. I think he stayed a couple of months. He did some work around the house, but the job I remember, carried out in the basement, was putting together a small dinghy from a kit. The pieces were formed plywood with lovely curves. There was a great deal of fitting and sanding, and he was the first to show me the use of woodworking tools, about which my father knew nothing. Earl would smoke a cigarette, forbidden in the house, while we worked and talked in the cavernous room below. I was part of the project, for it was to be my boat. I remember especially Earl's patience, as he drilled and screwed and caulked the pieces, and we began the endless sanding. After that, three coats of brilliant blue paint, and a springtime launch, I think after Earl had left. There were a first few trickles, then the boat swelled up tight as I rowed on the morning's high tide, down past the houses on our seafront road, as happy as I was ever to be.

Not many sons or daughters want to hear what their parents have done in bed—or perhaps worse, in bed with others. But I do. Sex drives all of us, and it drove my mother and father in ways I'm still trying to piece together.

Apart from his recent mention of fellatio, I've never heard Dad say a word about sex. He made no mention of the birds and the bees when I was growing up, and I've never heard him tell a joke with a sexual overtone. I think his natural reserve and circumspection is one reason women have always felt comfortable around him.

My mother went outside the marriage for more sex. I want to know when this started, and plumb my memories. Why was I so aware of an Austrian ski instructor she danced with on our Arlberg vacation, when I was seven? My father doesn't dance, and the instructor invited her out on the floor. An innocuous scene, surely, with my father and me sitting there—but why do I remember it, when so much else has faded? My mother was dancing with another man, and the implications of that must have struck me even then.

Who was the young man with a busted sports car who wound up staying at our house for a week when I was nine or ten?

Twenty years after my first meeting with Julio—the man who lit up my mother for four years, then left her—I met with him again in Miami, this time for a long meal in an ornate restaurant. He seemed larger and taller and more sure of himself, and more relaxed about me. I was in the middle of a book tour, clean-shaven and short-haired, traveling around to fifty cities in my van.

I asked Julio about the Austrian ski instructor, but my mother had never mentioned him. I asked if he knew when her affair began with Robert Capa. He didn't—but it must have been fairly early in my life, because Capa, while covering the war in Indochina, stepped on a land mine in 1954 when I was not yet twelve.

When I asked him, bluntly, about sex between my parents, he told me that for all the years of her marriage my mother had been careful not to make my father feel awkward in the bedroom. For him, sex was an act to be performed in the dark.

Nothing Julio ever told me came as much of a surprise. I already knew the bind my mother was in. She was married to a handsome, generous, considerate man, but one to whom sex, year after year, remained deeply embarrassing. One winter night in Vermont, when I was fifteen, I had a glimpse of this. We were staying at the Stowehof Lodge. My parents had disappeared before dinner and I went to track them down. I knocked on their door. I waited and knocked again but still no answer, so I turned the handle and went in.

All the lights were off. Then a sudden movement, a great rustling, and as my eyes adjusted to the dark I made out the two of them lying in one of the single beds, with my father straining to get as far away from my mother as possible—so far that his own torso, trapped by the sheet, sagged away from the bed, half-suspended above the floor. Finally, out of the near-dark, my mother's soft voice: "Why don't you and Alan go on into the dining room, and we'll join you soon."

I went downstairs and, exactly as my father would have done, told Alan nothing of what I'd seen. We sat in the dining room and ordered dinner, and after a while our parents joined us. The incident was already buried.

Julio remembered some stories about my mother's family. I learned that her father had lost his job teaching music at Ohio Wesleyan not because he was persecuted for his involvement with astrology—the party line I'd heard several times—but because of an illicit affair with a student.

I learned about my grandmother's courage when she stepped in front of my aunt's angry first husband and wound up with a broken leg.

I learned something I'd long suspected, that my mother liked to be dominated. She liked, more precisely, to have her bottom strapped.

There can't be many men in America who have heard such a report about their mother. But I was the one who had led Julio to the topic, after ruminating on something she had told me on that trip we took through Guatemala: *He dominated me completely, and I loved it.* That struck me when she said it in 1968, and thirty-five years later the words *domination* and *submission* had taken on a new and stronger flavor. By then I understood how my mother, an independent woman who took charge of her own career and her sexual life, might long for submission to someone more commanding than my father.

With *The Story of O* and *9 1/2 Weeks*, and the *Sleeping Beauty* books of Ann Rice, writing as A. N. Roquelaure, we've heard about the thrill of sexual and emotional submission. My mother must have felt it with Julio. Perhaps she loved having him decide everything—until the morning when she fixed him coffee and English muffins and he told her it was over. Submission carries its own risks.

Late in the evening after my dinner with Julio I walked out into the warm Florida night, got into my van and drove north on the interstate at eighty miles an hour, crushing waves of pale yellow bugs against my windshield. I drove and drove. It wasn't anger at Julio or at my mother for having an affair with him that kept me awake that night, but a tangential bitterness, a realization of what she had given up in order to have her men.

She always had a secret life. I understand that, because I've always had one of my own. As soon as I was a teenager I had desires I did not confess to anyone. But in that Florida night, as the yellow bugs slapped against my windshield, I saw how far my mother had gone to disguise her true nature, to keep a low profile and escape detection. I think she adjusted to my father's level of affection and pretended that was fine with her. She acted the contented wife, letting neither warmth nor animality show— which let her scud along with her affairs under the radar. The trouble for Alan and me was that she extended her reserve to us. She didn't curl up on the sofa with us, or climb into our beds, or sweep us into her arms.

It's a theory, I can't be sure of it. But I do know that she was riding out her marriage behind a scrim of propriety, when what she wanted was romance, sentiment and nights of wild submissiveness. Couldn't she have had all that and still been affectionate with her sons? I've been bitter about this, sometimes angry—but the more I know about my mother, the more I relax. What gnaws at me is *not knowing*. I'm not always sure what to do with the stories I uncover about my family, but I'm sure of this: if something happened, I want to hear about it. I figure it was all playing out, all the time, in what I could see going on, so I might as well know the truth. If I ever got to watch those *Truman Show* tapes of my parents' lives, I think my response would be sympathy and love.

When I was young my mother didn't talk about sex any more than my father did. But I knew her interest from the books she read. In my late teens she gave me not only Durrell's *Justine* but *Lady Chatterley's Lover*, after its long-awaited publication in an unexpurgated edition, as well as J. P. Donleavy's *The Ginger*

Man. She recommended Nabokov to me and Henry Miller, and later gave me a copy of Jorge Amado's sensuous Brazilian novel, *Gabriela*. Though these books were hardly graphic by today's standards, they opened up a world.

In the last forty years—during which I've had many girlfriends, fallen in love a half-dozen times and married once—I've paid lots of attention to sex. I can still feel restrained about the subject, but in my efforts *not* to feel restrained I've talked about it, read about it, and watched some pornography, most of it bad. I have a shelf of sexual volumes two feet long, from *The Joy of Sex* to Carol Queen's *Real Live Nude Girl*. I've read Shere Hite and Annie Sprinkle, Gloria Brame and Toni Bentley. These days women write the best books on sex.

Three years ago, after my breakup with Tasia Bernie, I lost most of my sexual interest. It disappeared and has barely started to return. I'm not worried about it, I'm taking a break—but no matter how tranquil I've felt about it here in my father's house, I think that over the years my perennial obsession with the topic has created a subtle rift between the two of us. Dad knows I'm like my mother, that I'm attuned to sex and emotion. He must know, too, that sex had a lot to do with why she left him. He may not want to think about his history with my mother, and my presence here could be a constant reminder. I know that whenever I see my own son, I see his mother.

It might not surprise him, given some of the scenes I've written, along with hints I've let out in print about my mother's love of being dominated, that I have a strong deviant streak myself. My perversions—this is the word I prefer—first surfaced in my mother's closet. Even before puberty I was aroused by her lingerie and underwear, and would sneak into her room when no one was in the house to try on her slips and bras. For twenty years I told no one this secret—a sure mark of shame—until it came clear to me that I was far from alone, that millions of other men have been aroused by cross-dressing, and many have cruised their mother's or sister's closets.

Then there's Tasia Bernie.

I'm a vanilla wafer next to that wild girl. She's a scholar, a graduate of Reed College and a lively writer, as fearless at a keyboard as in her six-inch heels. She moved from Oregon into my house in Ohio, bringing with her twenty boxes filled with books, clothes and kitchenware. The books filled my shelves, the clothes flew on and off her, and desserts started pouring out of my oven. "I have a baking disorder," she explained with a laugh.

I was in love with her confidence, with her perversions, with her unashamed pursuit of whatever aroused her. She had the courage I lacked when I was her age, and a huge sexual drive. Eventually she went back to Portland, where she wound up stripping at a woman-owned club and writing a blog about it. Some of this, without the libidinous details, I've told my father—and perhaps it's as clear to him as it is to me that Tasia links me to that other daring and sexual woman, my mother. Here is the heart of what divides us: if I'd been him, my mother is the one I would have loved.

After a full month I end my juice fast this morning, and find breakfast an unexpected disappointment. The same bowl of oatmeal and granola and banana that I've enjoyed for decades now has no flavor. Even worse, I chew a long-awaited blueberry muffin into a mass of gluten. All I can taste is the fats and binders as they cling to my gums. It's as if the fast has purified everything inside my mouth and there's no going back.

It makes me wonder what life will be like when I'm no longer looking after my dad. I think about the freedom of that the same way I thought about blueberry muffins: what a thrill it's going to be. Perhaps instead I'll feel adrift, and nothing will have any meaning. Perhaps *this* is all the meaning I'll find in life, this simple care I give my father.

It's rare for my father to initiate a conversation, but after dinner as I clear his plate he asks, "Who was that football coach . . . "

After he stalls I try to figure out what coach he's talking about. Was it someone we know, or a college coach, or someone in the pros? My father doesn't care about football, and without any leads I can only ask him questions that put him on the spot and get us nowhere. No wonder he doesn't want to talk anymore, because language defeats him every time. After I've grilled him, he stands up and goes into his room, retreating to the solace of his bed, and for the thousandth time I curse this disease.

I borrowed a wheelchair from the Council on Aging, convinced Dad to sit in it last night, and took him out for a roll down the bike path. It was dusk and the path empty, birds sang in the brushy woods, and the first hint of a fog was rolling in. With Dad facing forward I couldn't tell if he liked it or not. I loved it and told him I'd be happy to take him out twice a day, morning and night.

But today, when I make the offer after breakfast, he says "Not right now." At noon, "Let me think about it." And when I ask him again before dinner he seems to recoil in pain, as if I were pressing some onerous duty on him. He looks bedraggled these days, unshaven and worn out, and now I'm making him cringe. All he wants is to sit or lie inside, and for the hundredth time I give up on him. How can he not want to go outdoors? He might as well be living in a damn nursing home.

When I complain to Lois Gilbert about it she writes back, "Your dad is *busy*. It looks like sleeping all day to you, but he's in a limbo between life and death and it's like a baby sleeping in a crib right after birth—babies are exhausted from the ordeal of birth, and old people are exhausted from making the transition from life and lucidity to the black, mysterious, haunted void of death. It's like cramming for finals, or the most important exam of your life at a really hard school. You learn new reflexes, new ways of untangling the soul from the body. You begin to travel away from it, and take scary little field trips out of your home flesh and brain. Your dad's deepest consciousness is preparing for the ultimate leap of a long, adventurous life."

In 1935, when my father was in his first year at *Time* and exploring the possibilities of pictorial journalism, he bought one of the new lightweight candid cameras. That's what the publishing world called the small cameras that revolutionized photography in the thirties, enabling photographers to capture their subjects in candid poses—which is to say, no pose at all. The public showed an immediate appetite for such photos, and they had much to do with *Life*'s success.

August

Dad's camera was the best available, a German Leica that cost him $220, about a month's salary. He never took it out in the world much—it wasn't in his nature to poke into other people's lives the way the best of the *Life* photographers did—but he took endless photos of his own family. It's one reason why his folders are so thick. Though most of the pictures are pedestrian, he made a continuous record of us as we grew, from our first days until after we were in college.

My friend Geir Oslin has suffered from spina bifida all his life. His father died when he was nineteen, shortly after his mother became convinced that Geir was Jesus the Savior. She's still alive but has been institutionalized for decades. She's a 280-pound schizophrenic with diabetes and heart problems, and no longer gets out of bed. Geir tells me that occasionally he checks the online Social Security Death Index to see whether she's still alive. Going to see her can drop him deep into a depression, and other than some distant cousins he has no family.

"In a way," he writes me now, "I live vicariously through you and other people in regard to family. You have such a rich archive of several centuries of history to draw upon. I have not a single object or memento from my childhood. I don't even have a picture of myself younger than twenty-seven."

How bleak that sounds. All my life I've taken for granted the letters and photos and home movies and newspaper clippings that record my youth. But these exist only because my father collected and stored them. It's one of the hundred reasons why I love him.

Al and Ellen have arrived for our August reunion, and Janir and his wife will fly in at the end of the week. Al and I go right to work on the outdoor shower, and have an easy time of it: we always work well together. It's a comfort to me to see Al and his wife together. They've been married for thirty years, and their attraction to each other is stronger than ever.

The three of us and Harriet give Dad a little party, with barely a mention of the word *birthday*. Though he turned ninety-two last week, he has always tried to avoid any celebration or special attention on his birthday. For years I've phoned him on July 29 and said, "Hi Dad, just calling for no particular reason," to which he responds, "No, I can't think of any."

After dinner I tell the abbreviated story of how he started at *Time* straight out of college, stayed with Henry Luce for fifteen years and resigned that day in August 1949. In the week following that resignation, from our home in Connecticut, he wrote appreciative, individual letters to dozens of people he'd worked with at *Life*. Many of them wrote him back, and just a week ago I discovered a file thick with letters sent to him after his resignation. Now, at his no-particular-reason party, I read selections from them out loud.

All I wanted to say was that the joint won't
be the same for me—I have never worked for
a better managing editor or a nicer guy.

By the very fact that he holds the position, the
Managing Editor is in somewhat of an ivory
tower and I suspect that you never did realize
how firmly you held the respect and affection
of the staff. . . . Believe me, there is genuine
sorrow around here over your departure.

I just telephoned Oliver Jensen to find out what
happened. I told him I wanted to go up to your office
but I was afraid to go up without a Geiger counter.

It is not easy to say in a few words why you
like one man and dislike another, and it is
difficult to define why in your case I felt: this
is a man you can trust implicitly. The letter
you wrote me in December 1946, when my
son was killed, strengthened the sympathy I
always had for you. I am thinking of you all
the time since I read the notice in the *Post*.

I guess it's enough to say that, in my opinion,
few have been privileged to work for a fairer
person who tried to do an honest job.

I was never so shocked and stunned as on that
Monday when I heard of your resignation.
We did have fun on *Life*, didn't we?

There were many more, fifty-five in all.

Ellen offered to look after Dad this morning so I could
play an early nine holes with Al and the McGees, an annual out-
ing for me. Fun, but as we pulled back into our driveway, Ellen
stepped outside and I knew instantly there had been trouble.

Dad was sitting on the edge of his bed with his pants
around his ankles, shit on the floor, shit on his hands, shit in his
water glass.

"Don't come in," he said.

That had been enough to hold Ellen back, but Al and I waded
in. We moved him to the shower, we wiped and scrubbed and
eventually got everything cleaned up. Al even persuaded Dad
to accept his first complete shave in months, and by noon he
sat at the table in a striped blue and white shirt, fully shaved,
showered and combed, looking as spiffy as he has every other
August reunion.

Gerry Elovitz, the neuropsychologist, returned for a
reassessment and concluded, after a battery of tests, that Dad's
cognitive abilities have actually improved in the last six months.
This seems crazy to me, because in January I was having
paragraph-long conversations with my father.

But Dr. Elovitz, who last time pressed me to accept that my father would eventually have to live in some facility, now supported my plan to enroll him in Hospice and keep him at home. He spoke warmly of the Hospice nurses and doctors, and saw no reason why Dad couldn't die right here. This turned Al into a believer. Harriet has long been on board, and the next step is to get the approval of Dad's general physician. Though my father has no acute diseases, I can't believe he's going to live until Christmas.

Under Harriet's guidance we've chosen Hospice and Palliative Care of Cape Cod, one of several Hospice groups on the Cape. There are 3,300 separate Hospice operations in the United States, most of them qualified to receive funding from Medicare and Medicaid. Each is staffed by managers, doctors, nurses, home health aides and grief counselors—but the umbrella movement of Hospice is more a philosophy than an organization. Hospice is devoted to the comfort and dignity of its patients, rather than to curing or treating diseases. Its care is palliative: it seeks neither to hasten death nor to postpone it. In large part, Hospice is a reaction to the impersonal, technological maelstrom of hospitals, where the first concern is to *keep the patient alive*. There's a time for that, but such devotions can also prolong both patient and family misery.

Modern medicine is often genius. Its diagnostic and curative powers are vast, and my father has benefited from the attentions of his general physician, his heart and lung specialists, his dentist and podiatrist, as well as hospital technicians and staff. But at some point the cure looks worse than the condition.

Once Dad is signed up with Hospice, Medicare will cover most of his care at home. The catch is that it will no longer cover hospital visits or heroic interventions. It will cover ways to make him more comfortable, but not attempts at making him better. This is fine with us, because my father never wants to go back to the hospital anyway.

Janir and LL fly in on the red-eye from Denver, and I drive up to Boston to pick them up at 5:15 in the morning. They have only four days, I haven't seen them since their wedding over a year ago, and I can't get enough of them. We talk every minute of the drive home.

Al has agreed to look after Dad all through Janir and LL's stay, and that same morning we take off for the beach with Ellen, to meet up with various McGees, Posts and Ruschps—three other families with whom we often coordinate our August visits. There we eat, read and play volleyball, and dive into the cold ocean.

In the early afternoon Al gets some help from Harriet and comes out to join us for ninety minutes. Then back he goes. Perhaps he'll find Dad resting tranquilly, or perhaps a difficult evening awaits him, with Dad's body grown stiff, a contorted look on his face, a failing appetite, and the untraceable odor of urine in the bathroom. It's not that much work to look after Dad, but it's sobering, especially when everyone else is larking about.

At the end of the day Janir and LL and I stand on the Mc-Gees' second-floor deck, looking out over the ocean and the long white beach. The last of the Cape light is ebbing, and the sky turning rose. Hamburgers are ready on the outside grill, but we don't go down. Kids on their bikes ride past on the dirt road leading to other shingled houses on the bluff. It's summer, we're on vacation, we have stood here many times before and watched the day end, and for now there's nothing we have to do. We talk about beach plums and sunsets and a little about my dad's prognosis. My limbs are relaxing in a way I haven't felt since I came last December.

I've been reading James Salter's memoir, *Burning the Days*. "When was I happiest," he asks, "the happiest in my life?"

For me it was the years with my son on our farm in Ohio, years of volleyball and soccer in the living room, baseball in the meadow, board games at night and wasted hours with the rain falling outside and the two of us lying around on the sofa. It was a simple life—just as life with my dad is now simple and repetitive—but I was never more engaged than in those childhood years when Janir and I lived together.

Sometimes his mother would show up from California, with or without warning. Clarisa and I were divorced, and I'd had custody of Janir since he was three. She'd call us from the bus stop or the airport, and we'd pick her up. For a time she might be gentle and subdued, then erupt with fury at some slight or insult. She was unpredictable, she was a schizophrenic. Janir longed for her, I think, but had learned to be wary. She'd stay a week or two, then I'd buy her a ticket and we'd drive her back to the airport.

So there was heartbreak, even in those years. But mostly it was Janir and I together, day by day—and we were often in each other's arms. I took my cue from him, and that's what he wanted. Either I picked him up or he flung himself against my chest. Outside we had watergun fights, rotten tomato fights and raft tag at the pond, and at night our snuggled bedtime reading, a routine we never missed. I'd gone down a different path from the one my parents took, with no housekeeper, almost never a babysitter, and endless hours with my son. My mother and father had money, responsible jobs and each other. But there's nothing in the world I would have traded for my affectionate life with Janir. I think my parents missed out on plenty.

For thirty years Dad has been central to our August reunions, but this year he's barely part of it. People swirl past, he doesn't speak, I have no idea what he's thinking. These are my four free days, while Janir is here, and I pass by Dad in his chair with hardly a nod. He doesn't reach out to me, and now I don't reach out to him—because if I did, I'd wind up taking over the jobs I want Al to do.

I love being around my son, playing Ping-Pong, working on the shower, driving around to look for kiteboarding sites, his latest sport. There's no one on earth I'm more relaxed with than Janir. I still soak up how he smiles, how he cracks jokes, how he makes the whole table laugh by imitating my brother's serious and frequent delivery of the phrase, "That's *incredible.*"

Yesterday afternoon I drove Janir and LL up to Cambridge on their way to dinner and the airport. Before going to the restaurant, he and I took a stroll through Harvard Yard. It looked drab and trafficked, and standing in front of Hollis Hall, my freshman dorm, I found that I had no feelings about the place at all. Too many years gone by, perhaps. Or else the pleasure of walking around with my fond and curious son had simply displaced that ancient history.

Then out to dinner with two of LL's girlfriends from med school. They were a lively and knowledgeable trio, all busting ass through their long residencies. When my mother studied medicine only a handful of her classmates were women, and now the percentage is over half.

A good dinner, a rush at the end to get Janir and LL to the airport, and already I miss them.

There are days Dad gets up looking like he's wrestled with a bear all night, but this morning he rolls out of his room clear-eyed and chipper. "What's the program today?" he asks.

"Is there something you'd like to do?"

"I'd like to go to the beach."

Amazing. So after the usual routine of shower and breakfast, Al and I make some sandwiches, outfit Dad with his shoes, dark glasses and Australian sun hat, and get him into the car. The McGees have a permit to drive on the beach, so at their house we transfer Dad into their beach truck and drive down from Nauset Heights onto the sand, all the way out to the point, where a dozen of the young adults are sunning and reading. There's a swell of acknowledgment: Grandfather has come to the beach. Al and I lift and drag him along to a chair and ease him down into it. We set an umbrella over him and I put sunscreen on his face and hands, after which he settles back and promptly goes to sleep. No sandwich, no soda, no conversation, no watching the seals in the ocean or the girls tanning their perfect skin. He slumps down in the low-slung beach chair with his eyes closed.

My father loves the Atlantic. When he was a boy his parents took him each summer to Marblehead, where he learned to swim and sail and row. He has lived most of his adult life on the water, crossed the ocean on the old liners, swum in Maine's frigid bays and in the bathwater off Florida. He's taken his children and grandchildren to dozens of beaches, built endless sand castles with them and thrown his body in front of the waves to protect the ramparts—and now, though he's answered the call of the ocean once again, he's too tired to look at it.

While he sits and sleeps I join a volleyball game and play too long. By the time I check up on Dad, the heat and glare and wind have left him groggy, and he's past ready to go home. We hoist him back into the truck and I set off with him, leaving Al at the beach. From truck to car, no problem, but at home it's a battle to get him out of his car and up the ramp into the house. His legs shake and he can't move. Finally I step behind him, put my arm around his waist and lift him forward, one small shuffle after the next. He moans the whole way. "*Oh God. Oh Jesus.*"

We make it to his chair, and for the next six hours he lies in it. He's wrecked, but he has been to the ocean. Every time I think it's the last time, there's another time. It's still there, right now, waiting for us.

Before Al leaves we choose a little cremation plot at the Island Pond Cemetery, and buy it. Three by four feet, only $400, it can't get much simpler. Still, it wouldn't make Dad happy, and we don't mention it to him. He doesn't want to be buried anywhere, or for anyone to go to any trouble for him. Just throw his ashes in the ocean, he has told us. But I love this cemetery only a ten-minute walk from his house. It's hilly and wooded and quiet, with gravestones set among the pines and bush honeysuckle. Half Dad's ashes can go in the Atlantic off a beach raked by wind and pounding waves, but I also want a restful place where I can come and sit and think about him.

The reunion is over, the whole swirling crew has left the Cape, and there will be no more early-morning golf or tennis matches, no noisy evening cookouts, no card games or Ping-Pong. The house is quiet, which I like and which makes me sad. The cleaver of Labor Day is only three weeks away. We might have a lovely fall after that, but the richest days of summer are over, and I'm pretty sure it's my dad's last.

On August's hottest day my father lies in his chair, his socks off and his shirt unbuttoned. He's more curled than usual, which I take as a bad sign. I saw Oliver fold himself up in the months before he died, and I've read that it's a common symptom of late-stage dementia. Dad's breaths are shallow, his hands twitch and he has lost weight. Ever since his exhausting trip to the beach he has slept and slept.

He's thinner and more confused. He stands up from his chair, looks around and sits down again. The last of his interests are disappearing. He no longer cares what time it is, or what day of the month. He doesn't carry around his broken watch, or

John and Joe Thorndike, 2005

his wallet. Even his meals, those last holdouts of pleasure and promise, mean less to him. When I place a bowl in front of him, five minutes pass before he picks up his spoon and takes a bite. He's lost his memory, his agility, his sense of smell and four inches in height. On the other hand, he's held onto his hair and teeth and hearing and eyesight, and his perennial civility. He still never complains about anything.

       In the middle of the night I wake to desperate sounds from the monitor, run downstairs and find my father splayed half off his bed, fighting desperately to keep the back of his head from touching the floor. He's got one hand on the frame of his walker and the other on the lowered bed rail, and he's holding on with a look of rigid terror. Slowly I persuade him to let his head sink onto a pillow, and to relax his iron grip. Then I hoist him back onto the bed. He lies there stricken, breathing hard, his legs returning to their near-fetal position. When his breaths finally settle, he says, "Thank you."

I wake to hear Dad talking.

"Turn off the radio? Jane? *Jane?*"

It's the first time all year I've heard him say her name. I lie in bed in the dark, hoping for more, but that's it. He probably never wakes up, and I'm the one who can't go back to sleep. It's 4:26 in the morning and I'm lying in bed wide awake, thinking of the notes my father left Jane, and the one my mother left for him: *Thank you for your support. Your love, funny happy times—I shall miss you so.* Even after all my research, it's stunning how little I know about my parents' inner lives. I have these few slender hints, some scraps of ancient conversations, some photographs and letters. So few letters, really, and not one, all through their marriage, from my father to my mother. Whatever there was, I think Al threw away.

I should have come back to New York to help him clean out Mom's apartment, but I was wrapped up with Clarisa and Janir in Central America and let Al do all the work. By then he hated our mother, having suffered far more than I from her drinking and depression and barbiturate addition. It was Al who, as a teenager, had returned to her house one night in Sag Harbor and found her lying naked in the downstairs bathtub with the bathroom door open. She was taking a bath, she explained— but there was no water in the tub. It was Al, in his early twenties, who coped with her breakdowns when I was in El Salvador and distant Chile. And it was Al, some months after her funeral, who rented a U-Haul to cart everything away from her New York City apartment. He and a friend lugged all the heavy items down to the truck, but "at the end of the day," as he describes it, "we were just stuffing things down the incinerator flue. It was a nightmare of exhaustion, resentment, and anger at what Mom had put me through."

I don't blame him, I just miss what I think went down that flue. There must have been letters from her many friends, perhaps from Julio, certainly from my father. But none of that showed up in the small box of materials Al eventually passed on to me: a two-inch-thick folder with some letters I wrote her, some photos, a journal from her trip to India near the end of her life, and little else. And ever since, I've wanted to know more about her. I learned plenty in my two visits with Julio, but Mom lived for ten years after they broke up, and there's much more I'd like to hear. What, for example, happened to her work life in those years? I know one thing, that she developed "tennis elbow," a disastrous infirmity for an anesthesiologist in those days, because the flow of gas to an etherized patient was maintained manually via a bulb, squeezed by hand in a steady rhythm. Her bad elbow threw my mother out of the operating room, and eventually she signed up for a program at the University of Vermont for doctors who wanted to become psychiatrists. She moved to an apartment in Burlington, but found cold northern Vermont difficult. She was drinking, she was depressed, and she withdrew before the end of the first year.

It's a complex story, of which I know only the bones. What I want to hear is how she felt about her life, and about my father—and I think those papers that went down the flue could have told me a great deal.

Dad wakes up more slowly than usual, doesn't say good morning, isn't cheerful, doesn't move from his bed. Finally he admits that he doesn't feel well, though he can't explain why. Nothing hurts, he says, but his legs are stiff and his hands cold, and the color has gone from his lips. I start to rub his shoulders. I make a joke of it, saying that the Old Greek Masseur has come in for his morning rubdown. I put my hands on his neck and back. I'm actually giving his tight little body a massage, and he feels bad enough to accept it.

Dad's admission to Hospice is done. The nurse has come for her first visit, and he isn't happy about it. He doesn't understand why yet another person has to come to the house.

"To keep you out of the hospital," I tell him.

He can't argue with this, but he knows something strange is going on. He's right, because I haven't told him the nurse is from Hospice. He knows what Hospice is, and wouldn't want anything to do with it, wouldn't want to hear the word spoken.

I, on the other hand, am happy. I can already feel Hospice's support, their defense of a simpler death. Dad will die at home, and they will help. The nurse was relaxed. I made her a cup of coffee, and she drank it as she filled out her forms and began her journey into the center of our lives. She's a lively woman, perhaps fifty, divorced, drawn to this job years ago. It doesn't weigh her down, I can see. She knows death, and death is not so bad.

In the evening Dad sits in his chair, upright and motionless but not asleep. He looks like he could be meditating, though I'm sure he's never meditated before or had any interest in emptying his mind. My own mind wanders constantly, so I imagine that's what his is doing. But *thinking* might be too narrow a word to describe what goes on while he sits in his chair for ninety minutes, saying nothing. He's thinner and his hair has grown long, standing out around his angular face. He won't have it brushed or cut. He stares past me with an unnerving, disconnected look.

Finally he says, "Perhaps you could help me."

"Sure."

"I need to go . . . to that place . . ."

It takes me a few minutes to figure out that he wants to go to the supermarket. There must be something he needs there, but I can't figure out what. It's innominate, he struggles but can't describe it.

"I have to go," he says. "I have to be there." And finally a sentence that explains it all: "In case someone comes to the house."

He hates it when people come by, especially new people, and this will be his escape. Just going into his room doesn't get him far enough away, but if he goes to Stop & Shop—and stays there, I guess—he'll be safe.

Late in the afternoon I set the wheelchair next to my father, help him into it and head out for a walk on the bike path. We don't say anything. Though I can't see his face, Dad used to love the outdoor world, and I believe it still rouses him. He seems alert to the sunshine, to the breeze and the call of the crows. I love these walks. Guiding his chair forward, almost without effort, I think about the two of us. I think this: that I was born and grew up in his best years, and that my early childhood—such a sunny and carefree time for me—came in his thirties, during his great success at *Life* and the early years of his marriage to my mother. The happiness we both knew then remains a bond between us, and I feel it now as we glide over the silky asphalt past the scrub pines and the town's blue water tank. These quiet walks, these days we spend together are not the high point of his life, nor of mine, but we are joined until he dies.

September

Jane's daughter Catherine drives to the Cape for a visit. Dad breaks into a smile as soon as she enters the room, but Catherine hasn't seen him in a year, and the shock on her face shows how much he has aged. She walks up to him and stands beside him, puts her arm around him, kisses his head again and again. She doesn't say anything, but starts to cry and for a long time can't stop.

Anyone who loves my dad, I love.

I've hired Marion Prendergast, a woman I met at the Council on Aging, to come over twice a week so I can get out of the house and do something athletic. At first I worried about how Dad would get along with her, because he doesn't like a new face. During her first few visits he slept a lot and they spoke little, but yesterday they had a breakthrough in communications, as Marion put it. She fixed the air purifying machine that's supposed to run constantly in the living room, and that led to some talk, at which my father woke up to her. Indeed, when I returned from my Sunday bike ride his mood was cheerful bordering on electrified. He smiled, he was attentive, and when Marion said good-bye and went out to her car, Dad got on his walker and followed her out to the driveway. This, from a guy I can rarely persuade to leave the house.

For the rest of the day he remained alert. He expressed an interest in the John Adams biography by David McCullough that lay on the dining room table, and I handed it to him. For almost an hour he wandered around the house, sitting down with the book on his lap, then standing up again and resting it on top of his walker as he looked around the kitchen, looked around his room. Finally he sat down and asked for a notebook and pen. Over the next hour he wrote several lines, and later I took a look at them.

> Jensen material right dad
> Shoes
> Joe Boyd Do I have material from him

That was more than he'd written in months. Though lacking punctuation, there was even a complete sentence. His mind was ticking over, he had projects, he later announced, "I think I'm going to go so far as to have a cocktail," and under his scrutiny I poured him a stiff one. He took only a few sips from it, but after dinner he kept moving, inspecting his desk and his photos on the living room walls. When I retired at ten he was still sitting upright in his chair, uninterested in sleep.

I don't think it's irrelevant that Marion is a tall, engaging, well-spoken woman. A woman who says *tomahto* for the vegetable, and *ahnt* for her mother's sister. She is also quite attractive, as well as light-haired. My father's natural draw is to blondes, and I doubt that has changed with age. *Something* lit him up for twelve hours straight.

Consider an incident from our August reunion, when another blonde was in the house, Janir's wife LL. She and Janir were sleeping in the little room above the laundry. In the middle of the night Janir woke to rattling and shuffling, and found his grandfather halfway down the three stairs between kitchen and laundry room. He had his walker with him and was trying to negotiate the second tread, something he hadn't done in six months. He was confused, he was worried about them, perhaps they needed something. Or perhaps he needed something. All we know for sure is that the ancient male was roaming his terrain.

I come down in the morning to find Dad awake, lying in bed with a troubled face.

"I had the most terrible nightmare," he says.

I sit on the little trunk at the foot of his bed and ask him what happened.

"I dreamed my father died."

I put my hand on his feet, wanting to console him. He has the worried look of a child. He searches my face, then asks, as if fearful of the answer, "Is there any truth to that?"

"It's true, Dad. It happened many years ago."

He looks stricken by this news. Almost fifty years have passed since his father's death, but grief overwhelms him now. I've never seen him look so unprotected and forlorn. An hour passes before he comes around.

Sandy calls to tell me his father has died, at ninety-six, and I ask him the question he always asks me: "How do you feel?"

"Relieved, I guess. And guilty. I had another great bawling catharsis, the same as with my mother. But you know I wanted them to die and leave me that money. I never hid it. I thought they'd lived long enough. So fear, too, of what people will think of me."

"It's not like you put them on an ice floe. You did everything you could to make them happy and comfortable. You did that for years."

"I did. But no matter how long it goes on, you're not supposed to want them to die. Of course I think a lot of people do and can't admit it. I think a lot of old people are ready to go, but *they* can't admit it. I wonder how many would push some button if they could, and just end it. Is your father still interested in life?"

"A little less all the time."

"Would he have wanted to live this long? In the condition he's in?"

"Absolutely not." I'm sure of this, though less sure of how he feels now that he's closer to the end. "Don't all of us say the same thing," I ask Sandy, "that if we're too debilitated we wouldn't want to live? But maybe that's just what we think now, and later we'll change our minds. I'm pretty sure my father has. He's probably looking around and thinking, *Hey, it's this world or nothing*— and he'd rather have something. I can imagine myself going through the same change. Right now I'd say, *Shoot me, get rid of me*. But when I get close, who knows? How about you?"

"I'll fight it tooth and nail," Sandy says. "I love this life and I won't want to go. I'll tell them to do everything they can think of to keep me here."

Emerging from his shower, my father no longer dries himself off. He just waits for me to help, then makes low quavering noises as I rub his scalp and chest, his skinny arms and legs, the hollows below his collarbones. He's frail and forgetful. He sits down for breakfast and eats so slowly he seems to draw a blank as he holds his spoon. Once seated in his lift chair he stares straight in front of him. All day he sits and breathes. He's on his last legs, and the question keeps coming back to me: What's the point of such a minimal life?

Make a jump with me here to the two years I spent in the early seventies, living with my wife and young son on a backcountry farm in Chile. Our neighbors were hardworking peasants with small decent houses and enough to eat, who lived far more pedestrian lives than the friends Clarisa and I had left behind in Boulder. But as we settled into Chilean country life, it became clear to me that our neighbors there were no different from anyone else. They were driven by the same emotions, they suffered and celebrated in the same ways, and their lives were worth no less than my own.

Of course, how obvious. But when you're born in Manhattan, grow up in a privileged segment of the world's richest nation, attend a New England boarding school and top it all off with four years at that thoroughly elitist institution, Harvard, it's easy to be tainted by the idea that the lives of some potato-planting campesinos in southern Chile are somehow less valid than your own.

Now jump back to my father, sitting down on the toilet so I can work his pants up over his ankles. My father, who claims every day that he can button his own shirt, but who can't. My father, who periodically shits on the floor, who can't hold a conversation, who may not know whether he's in pain or not. What's the point, I ask myself, a half dozen times a day.

But my dad's life is his own. It may be less of a life than the rest of us have, only a small reed of a life—but he is driven by the same emotions, knows suffering and has his pleasures. He's alive and wants to stay alive, and until that changes there's no way I could slip him any of those Nembutals.

Kathy Galt and Billy Renz have come to visit, driving all the way from Ohio. I love that they've made the effort, and how they link my two worlds.

One of Kathy's skills is drawing people out, especially old people. She's done some interviewing for the local NPR station, and she can get almost anyone to talk. But in my father she meets her match. She sits at the dining room table with him, brings him food and shows that she's interested in what he has to say. But conversations with my dad are thin affairs. This morning she took him out for a walk on the bike path in his wheelchair— an expedition I set up for them because of how much I love that walk myself. But after wheeling him along for a few hundred yards, Kathy stopped to check on him, to see how he felt about it. He looked a little worried, she thought.

"I tried to put myself in his place," she told me when they got back. "What if my memory was failing and someone I didn't know was pushing me along past all that waving vegetation, in and out of the shadows, and the world kept coming at me? It could be scary. It could be like a trip on mushrooms or something. I tried to sink into his world, to feel how disorienting it could be not to know where you'd come from or where you were going. I thought he might be struggling with it, so I brought him back."

Still, she finds Dad charming. We're all sitting around after dinner, talking about Iraq and Iran, when he comes out with a perfectly clear sentence. "It's hard to slow down a president bent on war."

"And we have one of those, don't we?" Kathy says.

"I'll show you." Dad pulls his walker to him and rises to his feet. "I'm going over here, and I'm going to roll. You try to stop me. You'll see how hard it is, once I get going. It's like a snowball rolling down a hill, going bigger and faster. You try to stop me."

Kathy and Billy both look at me. I shrug: I don't know what he's doing. But I'm standing close by when he starts to lower himself to the floor, and grab his arm to help him down. Soon he's stretched out on his back, legs extended and ready to start rolling. "Try to stop me," he tells Kathy, who squats beside him. He tucks one elbow under his side and begins to roll toward her.

"Oh," he says, and stops. "I can't do that."

Now he looks confused, as if he has no idea what he's doing on the floor. The three of us lift him to his feet and guide him to the Monstrosity. He has no more explanations, though Kathy plies him with questions. For thirty minutes she hovers on the edge of laughter.

"That was so cute," she says later. "What was he doing? Was he the president, or was that the army, or what was that? You can see he's thinking about things."

What a spirited group we've been. Kathy talks politics, Billy cooks, and my father gets to see a different side of me as I argue and laugh, even scream in the dining room as I do my imitation of Bruce Springsteen from his 1977 concert in Athens. "*I am a prisoner,*" I cry, then leap up in the air and come down with a phantom guitar and Springsteen's exuberant howl, "*of rock and roll!*"

Then, to really liven things up while my friends are here, Joe Jr. and two-year-old Eliza arrive for a visit. Eliza's the one for Dad. In his ideal world, I think, she'd come to visit every day. And she's fascinated by him. She drapes herself over the padded arms of his lift chair, stares at him when he's sleeping, wants to go into the bathroom when he's seated naked on the toilet and I'm drying his toes with the hair dryer.

In the afternoons Joe takes care of both Eliza and Dad while the rest of us go to the beach, empty and swept by a new cold wind, the sand stinging our ankles as we watch the seals watch us. Kathy puts on a wetsuit and swims out to them, but they keep their liquid-eyed distance. Life is rich like this, with lively people in the house, help with Dad and long walks with Billy to the point.

How lucky I was with Janir through his teenage years. There are kids who pull away from their parents, who don't want to be seen around them or touched by them. It happens to all kinds of families, it can't be foretold, it almost seems the luck of the draw. But with Janir, at least when we were home, we always found ways to be close. I didn't put my arm around him outside Boulder High, where his friends would see, or on a ski lift at one of his downhill races. But we still read together at night, still played soccer-shoot-on-goal in the living room, still wrestled. He'd slam me from behind at I entered my room, hurling me onto the bed with a linebacker cry of "Administer the hit!" We'd scramble around and pin each other against the wall, and after a while relax and just lie there arm in arm.

One day during his junior year, after a prolonged battle in which I kept escaping his hold—he couldn't pin me, I kept squirming my way out—I stopped and gave him a look. "Janir, are you sandbaggin' me?"

The faintest smile—then he leapt on top of me and in three seconds had me pinned. After ten I stopped struggling. "Damn, is this how it is now? You just toy with me?"

"Dad," he said, smiling broadly, "I'm young and strong."

On Sunday nights we watched television, not so much for the movies with their endless ads as for the chance to lie around in a dead time and do nothing together, our arms and legs touching.

When Janir started at the University of Colorado I moved down to Santa Fe, in part to let him have his time "away" at college. I came back to see him several times during the fall, we spent Christmas in Vermont, and we went skiing in February— but when I drove up to visit him in March he was busy. He had homework, a Sunday ski race at Winter Park, and scrubwork at a fraternity he was pledging. On Saturday afternoon, in our last half hour together, we stretched out on the rug of our old Boulder apartment in front of the TV and watched a hockey game. It was a way to lie side by side and not talk. But I had something to say. I hadn't seen enough of him and wanted to tell him how glad I was to have this quiet time together. I found it awkward to say, but slipped my arm around his shoulders and finally came out with it: "I'd hate to come up and not get to lie around like this the way we used to. At least for a few minutes. I know you're busy and you're growing up—but I still love to hold you."

The game droned on in front of us. For a moment I thought he wasn't going to say anything. Then he shifted his weight closer and said, "Always hold me."

Everyone goes back to Ohio and Virginia, and I wake this morning later than usual with the room already light and the sound of a small motorboat going by outside. I'm a young boy waking up in my house on Long Island Sound with a rapturous summer day before me.

A massage therapist once told me, "If you could wake up some morning and feel what your body was like when you were young, you would be *so* unhappy. Because you'd realize how stiff all your joints have become."

The sound isn't a motorboat, it's a lawnmower, and I'm not a young boy. I'm a sixty-two-year-old man lying in bed in my father's house, wishing I could wake up as that lucky young boy.

When I write that, *a sixty-two-year-old man*, it doesn't sound like me at all, not one bit.

It could have happened when I was out mowing the lawn, or off at the hardware store picking up some paint, or out rollerblading on the bike path. Instead it was early in the evening and I was sitting at the dining room table—and still I couldn't prevent it.

WHAM.

I ran into Dad's room and found him stretched out on the floor with his walker folded up beneath him. Already there was blood, and he moaned hard when I pulled the walker out from under him and rolled him over. His face was scrunched up and his hair slick. Blood everywhere, already pooling on the floor, and I couldn't be sure about the wound because hair and flesh and blood were all mixed up together. I pressed a towel to the side of his head, removed the cloth and saw an inch-long gash, or perhaps just a flap of skin. Bleeding is trouble for anyone taking a blood thinner, so I kept pressure on the towel. I broke only to pick up the telephone and dial Hospice. I got an operator, who said a nurse would call me back.

October

By the time she did I'd replaced the towel with some gauze from a packet, then applied more gauze, and slowly the blood stopped seeping through. My father was still on the floor with a pillow under his head, his eyes closed and his arms clenched over his chest. "Don't disturb the bandage," the nurse said. "If the bleeding has stopped he'll probably be all right. We'll come over in the morning and butterfly it, and try to keep him out of the hospital." All of us have the same goal.

Eventually I hauled him up onto his bed and stretched him out. The gauze pads stayed on his head as I attended to scrapes on his wrist and elbow and shin. Dad barely said a word the whole time, but admitted he felt sore. I lay a pack of frozen peas, wrapped in a dishtowel, against the side of his head, and an hour later, when he finally drifted off, I lay down on the living room couch under a blanket, keeping an ear out to make sure he didn't wake in the night and try to make it to the portable commode in his room, or even to the bathroom. After the drama of his fall, it was a couple of hours before I drifted off to sleep.

Dad's new cardiologist wants him to go to the hospital and have a CT scan. After a fall like that, his nurse explains, there could be bleeding inside his skull. But our new Hospice nurse, Deb Leo, looks Dad over and says, "The guy's doing okay. We're not going to take him anywhere." After all, if they found bleeding on his brain, what could the doctors do? Nothing my brothers and I would accept, at this point. I know mainstream medicine must take every precaution, but we're past that now. We're in the hands of Hospice, and they support Dad's refusal of all hospital care.

Since his fall my nights of easy sleep are over. I used to go to bed upstairs and let him make his own nighttime trips to the bathroom and back, but now I can't shake the vision of him lying on the floor with a pool of blood under his head. So I've replaced the couch in the living room with a bed, and that's where I sleep. Every time Dad puts his feet on the floor and reaches for his walker, I wake up and go in to help him. I've finally persuaded him to use the commode in his room, but once settled there, five or ten minutes pass before he's finished peeing, and the longer he takes, the more I wake up. Finally he's ready. I help him stand up and escort him the five steps to his bed, and soon I'm listening to his snores as I lie in my own bed, miles from sleep.

Eventually I drop off, but two hours later he reaches for his walker, I hear the rattle and wake up again, and we go through the same operation.

On the third night I ask him if he can stay in his bed so I can sleep. "You could just pee in your underwear," I explain cheerfully, "and we'll change it in the morning."

"Well, I guess that's all right with me."

I stash his walker in the dining room so he won't forget his promise—and an hour later jump up to the sound of his plastic water glass hitting the floor. With no walker, he's got one hand on his bedside table and the other on the wainscoting, and his legs are shaking like an aspen. He looks vulnerable and lost, but no easy wave of love washes over me. Though I'm outwardly patient and do the right thing, all I can think of is how tomorrow by noon I'll be falling asleep on my feet.

Only four days of this and I'm moving like a zombie. Two more days and I'm collapsing. I have to find some nighttime help. I make some calls and come up with a group of four women, all with plenty of experience with the old and infirm. Bambi and the Eldercares, I call them, and Bambi and I set up a schedule for Monday through Saturday nights. It seems profligate to hire someone to come in and stay awake all night for what amounts to about an hour of work—but I can no longer do it on my own.

Dad hates having someone in the house all night. I don't really like it myself, but as soon as I start getting enough sleep in my room upstairs I recover from my desperation. Now I feel fine, and six nights a week I have help. On Sundays, to keep my hand in, I sleep in the living room and get up whenever Dad does.

In less then a week I'm supposed to start my break. Al is coming for ten days and I'm driving back to Ohio.

Dad can no longer reach the commode on his own, and even when I help him it's touch and go. I try to stand him up next to the bed so he can support himself with the walker, but when I lift him up, either his knees buckle or his legs go stiff and his feet slide across the floor.

I hate to lift anything early in the day. By eleven o'clock I can move stacks of drywall with impunity, even bags of concrete, but early in the morning I might strain my back just taking out the garbage. Right now it *is* early in the morning, and Dad needs to use the commode. I try getting behind him and lifting, but his legs keep sliding away. Finally I dispense with the walker, wriggle off his pants and underwear, circle him around the waist and lift him bodily, making the pivot from bed to commode. His arms and legs go rigid. He shakes and cries out *No! Where am I going? Oh God. Where do I sit?* I succeed in landing him on the plastic seat.

Once he has tinkled into the bucket I take advantage of his position to give him a quick sponge bath. I reach under him and swab away under his testicles and farther back, trying to clean around his anus. It's hard to tell exactly where I'm wiping, but at least I've given the area a pass with a warm wet towel.

Marion tells me about a back-saving maneuver in which you squat in front of the patient, put his arms around your neck, then lift with your legs and pivot him off the bed onto the commode or wheelchair. "Nine out of ten patients will clutch onto you when you start to lift them," she says, and claims she moved a woman last year who weighed twice what she does. But Dad must be the one in ten. He can't seem to grasp one wrist with his other hand, and if I do it for him and then slip my head under the circle of his arms, he panics and lets go the minute I start lifting. He's terrified, he cries out, his limbs go stiff and he's no help at all.

I think he's had his last shower. I wouldn't dare take him into the bathroom now—it's far too tight in there.

Bambi comes over at night, which gives me a good sleep, and together we get Dad on and off the commode in the morning. Now he's had some breakfast, but I'm a mess. I did far too much lifting yesterday and wound up straining my back. I can still walk around, but I have to stop picking Dad up and moving him from bed to chair, or even onto the toilet. At noon I'll have some help from Jerry, one of the home health aides from Hospice, and Marion will stop by tomorrow. Harriet is off at her camp.

I send Al an e-mail, warning him of how things stand: "There could be some tough sledding around here when you come. I've thought about not going out to Ohio, but I still want to. I talked to Deb about it, she thinks I should go. I doubt if I'll know until the last minute. I could always hustle back."

The Hospice aides are great. Alison, the gentlest of them, is dark-eyed, calm and always beautifully dressed. In some other life she's an artist, with a husband and two teen-aged children. Here she enters the house with her thick dark hair pulled back and her hands clasped before her. She says a few soft sentences to my father and wins him over with her calm and reserve.

Jerry is married, has raised five daughters, and in some previous incarnation worked twenty years for General Electric. He could still be holding down a corporate job, but he's had enough of that world and now looks after people who are dying. "Your dad is easy," he told me the last time he was here. "I've got a three-hundred-pound guy who's paralyzed from the waist down. He's got cancer of the spine, and the worst part of it is—I can't cheer him up!" It's a joke, but Jerry's serious: he wants to make people laugh, to sing songs and tell stories and bring some life into the house. He's another gabber, and I feared he'd get on my father's nerves, but he doesn't. He walks in the door and says, "There's three guys in a bar"—and Dad winds up laughing at the joke. I love Hospice, and so far everyone in it.

Just before Jerry arrives, Dad craps mightily in bed, his first bowel movement in three days. I let Jerry do the cleanup, but help out so I can see how it's done. First we stand Dad up next to the wall, holding onto a new grab bar, and Jerry tears away the heavy paper underwear, wiping him behind, then in front, saying repeatedly, "I know, I know," an acknowledgment of the humiliation and pain of a job that must be done. Dad still has choices—he can eat or not, he can speak or not—but there's no choice about this, because he's going to be cleaned up. As we work at it I keep thinking he's going to dig in his heels like a stubborn New England cuss. But he doesn't. He seems to have accepted that now he has a new life in which he lies in bed, with an occasional trip to the commode four feet away. As far as I can see, he still wants to live.

I've gone to Athens and returned, and when I walk back into the house I find Al cleaning up our father in bed, a job he now knows better than I: how to roll Dad from side to side with a draw sheet to remove the wet or soiled bed pads beneath him, how to get his underwear off and on, how to protect the bedsore at the base of his spine. Dad is now incontinent, both bowel and bladder, and no longer leaves his bed.

Once again Al has had a good stay. Even with Dad declining into stillness and silence, there's a peacefulness in the house that Al welcomes. I feel it as soon as I come in. I've had my vacation, talked to my friends, paraded on Court Street with twenty thousand Halloween revelers, and now I'm back to my real life.

Al feeds Dad his dinner in bed, spooning in a few bites of lasagna before moving on to Starbuck's Coffee Almond Fudge. Ice cream is all he really wants. It slides down smoothly, and a

November

few hours later he's ready for more. Al and I talk in the kitchen about how long he might last. No one can say. Hospice can't say. His shoulder and ankle bones protrude, his legs are thinner than ever, and we're careful when we move him, fearful of snapping a bone. He's dying now, day by day, in Al's hands, in my hands, in Harriet's hands. After Al leaves I tell the night sitters to come every other evening, and start sleeping in the living room the nights they're not here.

I read what the Hospice guidebook has to say about the last stages of life, as the body and mind shut down: how death is a gift for both the person dying and those taking care of him. But the gift for me is Hospice itself.

My country can seem so shameful, with its warmongering and imbalance of wealth, and neither the military nor any politician ever stirs me to patriotism. But Hospice does. That there is a group like this, that these people have helped so many die with grace, makes me proud of my beautiful nation and everyone in it. I know that Hospice started in England and exists in many other countries—but this is the Hospice and palliative care I know, one recognized by our government and largely paid for by Medicare. So now I sing praises to my country.

My father is not the island he used to be. People are touching him all the time, and he seems to accept it. Harriet and I massage his shoulders, his arms and legs. I work on his feet to maintain his circulation, especially his heels where the risk of bedsores is high. Touch flows to him now as it flows to an infant, and all the aides have their hands on him. I rub his scalp or work some lotion into his shins as he grunts and makes small noises I can't interpret, but which don't sound like objections.

A range of emotions plays across his face. When I rub him he grimaces, occasionally smiles, sometimes gives a look of confusion. When I roll him to his left I see his fear of falling. He doesn't talk about his feelings any more than he used to, but they're more visible now. And this, I realize, isn't new: all year he's been losing the ability to hide his emotions.

Don't explain, don't complain. That was Cole Porter's credo, and could have been my father's. Yet now I remember how distraught he looked after dreaming that his father had died. I think of his crazed expressions when I found him lying between the toilet and the wall, and his great frustration when he tried to carry on a conversation and could not, and the defeat that drowned his face—his whole body—after his first evaluation by the neuropsychologist.

I've seen his troubles, but also the joy on his face when Jane's daughter Susie called him on the phone, and when her other daughter, Catherine, came to visit. I think of his elation, his pure glee at playing hide and seek with his granddaughter Eliza. Though his memory and language have given way, he's been showing me plenty of how he feels. His face is mobile and his emotions roll over it, he can't hold them back. I've been too literal, waiting for sentences that are now beyond him. I give up on them. I don't need them. I rub his body and watch his face, and I talk to him.

I tell him stories. I slip the headset over his ear when Al or young Joe calls. When I tell him it's my birthday, he brightens. "Is it?" He speaks less and less, but he can still make a joke. After a single bite of butternut squash last night he turned his mouth away. "Okay," I said, "we could dispense with this and go straight to the coffee almond fudge."

"I've heard of that," he said.

Humor and good manners: it's amazing how long they hold up.

Harriet comes over, Alison comes or Jerry comes, and for two or three hours a day I have help. The rest of the time the house is still. Dad sleeps and sleeps. Sometimes I pull a chair up beside his bed and watch him. If he wakes he might stare at me before closing his eyes again, and in those moments I have the uncanny feeling that *he*'s the one looking after *me*. It's the habit of a lifetime, that he's the father, that I'm safe with him, that I can make mistakes and he'll still be here for me.

All year I've thought about Sandy Weymouth's advice: *If it were me I'd leave him alone. I wouldn't do anything until he asked, and then I'd do everything.* This wouldn't work now, but what intrigues me is to see how close this comes to my father's ideas on parenthood. It's what he always did: let me choose my way, and helped out in any way he could.

Sandy Weymouth and my father: could any two men be further apart on the question of emotions? In Dad's files I've found a carbon copy of a letter he wrote me years ago, after I sent him a copy of Sandy's book.

> I am not the right reader for Sandy Weymouth's manuscript. As we have discussed before, I am not enthusiastic about the uninhibited expression of all one's personal feelings. If everyone told everyone else exactly what we thought of each other, I am afraid we would all end up at each other's throats. The conventions of polite social discourse, however artificial and insincere they may sometimes seem, serve the purpose of allowing people to interact peacefully and productively.
>
> As a child of the Enlightenment, I believe that human progress—even survival—depends on the assertion of man's reason over his animal instincts. The skin of civilization is very thin and when it is torn anywhere, the furies may be let loose. Only men of reason can bring us safely through the

coming age of nuclear proliferation. I take as my role models Thomas Jefferson and Pliny the Younger.

Cogent, isn't he? It's the very opposite of Sandy's belief that, to our detriment, reason has crushed the cathartic expression of our feelings. Yet Sandy and my father are joined in their dislike of coercion. They both believe in letting a child—or an adult son—follow his own lead. For as long as I can remember, Dad's underlying advice to me has been the same: *Live your life, the one you want.* Instead of imposing his own ideas, he supported whatever I chose to do.

When I married a woman from El Salvador who convinced me to spend a Colorado winter in a tent high above Boulder, and who refused to consult an obstetrician when she was pregnant, I never saw any judgment on my father's face or heard it in his letters. He didn't throw his arm around Clarisa when they met, but he was always gracious and attentive to her.

When I was busted on the New Jersey Turnpike with a bag of pot and some LSD, he found a lawyer for me and never said a word of reproach.

When I divorced, he said he was sorry to see it happen, but of course I knew best.

When I raised my son on my own, and farmed when there was no money in it, and started books that didn't work out, he let me find my way. He watched, apparently unworried, as I ate the full sixties meal: drugs, communes, farming, single father-hood, protests against the war, long hair, wild parties and free love. It was all his fault, I once told him as a joke. He was the one who'd first shown me Allen Ginsberg's *Howl*, which led me to the beatniks, and it was all downhill from there.

When I started writing novels, though he was never interested in fiction himself, he read the manuscripts and made helpful comments. I'm sure the sex scenes made him uncomfortable, but he never suggested I take them out.

When I gave him Sandy's book on Emotional Work, he read every word.

When Janir was sixteen and I wanted to go to Mexico to do some research, Dad came and lived my life for me in Boulder. He looked after Janir, drove him to baseball games after school, even took in Clarisa when she showed up unannounced to visit her son.

If I talked about my mother, he didn't cut me off. If I published an article in which I described going to meet her lover, he didn't complain. He let me pursue what was vital to me. If I wanted to be a different kind of man, someone unlike himself—that was fine, he believed in that. He believed in letting me choose. He wasn't everything I needed in a father, but everything he could give me, he did.

All this was in my bones, so when Janir was growing up I tried to do the same for him, to let him live the life he wanted. It sounds easy but it's not, because there were times, such as the day he quit his soccer team, when I was sure I knew what was best for him.

His junior year at Boulder High, playing for a coach he couldn't stand, he lost his starting position. To me Janir looked as skilled as any player on the field, quick to the ball and utterly fearless. But week after week, the coach rarely played him. Was I wrong in thinking that the Anglo kids played more, and the other players—the Mexicans, the Vietnamese and Cambodians—spent more time on the bench? It was hard to tell, a black kid was one of the stars. But after a home game in which Janir only got in for a couple of minutes at the very end, he bagged the team meeting, wouldn't look at me, and walked straight to our car in the lot. He was finished.

I tried to persuade him not to quit. If he wanted to play varsity, with a different coach, he had to get through JV. Next year would be different, I assured him.

I drove him home, where he flung his cleats and shin guards into the corner. "Fuck next year. I've gone to every single practice and busted my ass for two minutes a game. I play better than half the guys out there and I'm sick of it."

Still I argued. He couldn't just quit, he had to stick it out.

He *could* quit, he said. He stood facing me, his hands on his hips, defiant. "You know why? Because I do what I *feel* like."

I loved that from the moment he said it, and later had some T-shirts printed up. There's one upstairs now, in my closet.

I Do What I Feel Like
—Janir

He can be a wonderfully stubborn little cuss. And now I see how much his confidence in his own decisions is actually a legacy passed down from my father. Live your life, Dad told me—and now my son embodies that. I realize this as if someone had just tapped me on the forehead, and now it's all I see: this chain, this braided rope that holds us together.

After consulting with Deb Leo, and with my dad's GP and cardiologist, Harriet and I have withdrawn almost all Dad's medications: the Coumadin, the Prozac, the Aricept and others. Only Cartia is left, to regulate his heartbeat. Harriet still comes every day. She approaches Dad's bed with the same cheery "Hi, Joe, how're you doing?" and he responds with the same "Getting along pretty well." Every time Harriet walks into the house she's a comfort to me, and I'm sure to my dad as well. All the books say, *You cannot do this alone,* and it's true.

Dad sleeps fitfully. He kicks off his covers, pushes down his underwear, sometimes grips the rails of his bed. He rarely drops under so far that I can't wake him with the softest inquiry. "Dad?" I say, at any time of day or night, and immediately he opens his eyes. Perhaps, I've thought, it's pain that keeps him from a deeper sleep. So two days ago, after talking to Deb Leo about it, I gave him his first oxycodone, half a five-milligram tablet. That's a light dose, but he's a "narcotic naive" and the effect was dramatic. Forty minutes after swallowing the pill he was too dazed to finish eating his ice cream, and five minutes later he was fully asleep. His breathing stayed shallow but steady, and for seven straight hours he didn't move.

It seemed a glorious rest, but there's been a tradeoff. An old obsession overwhelmed him yesterday when Deb stopped by to see him: something was wrong near the foot of the bed, and he needed to know what it was. "Down there, I have to go down there. Can you help me get down there? Please, help me go down there. Please, can't you do that?"

Nothing appeased him, no words or explanations. Finally we cleared the table and dresser from the far end of the room and turned his hospital bed around so his head was close to the bookshelves. Now he looks toward the doorway. He used to face west, the traditional direction of death, and now faces east.

Tonight, when I return from tennis at eight, Marion reports that he's been anxious and has begged repeatedly for help. He wants to get out of his bed, to get out of his room, to get out of the house. She warns me he might slide off the end of the bed or somehow climb over the rails. "I've seen patients who couldn't move at all," she says, "and all of a sudden something comes over them and they climb right out of the bed and land on the floor."

At nine I give him another dose of the oxycodone. I go to sleep in the living room, wake at two to check up on him, and find that his position hasn't changed. It isn't until four-thirty that he begins to rustle around. I wake again, get up, clean up his behind as he lies curled against one of the rails, then try to soothe his rising distress. He pleads with me, as he did with Marion. He clutches my hand and asks for help. "I need to get out of here," he tells me. "Out of here. Help me, please, I need to get out of here. Please help me. Please, please, please help me get out of here."

I've never heard anything like this from my father. His face is drawn and he grips my hand with his own. He doesn't want to wear his Depends and keeps working them down off his legs. His teeth chatter, his voice quavers and disappears and grows louder again, and his anxiety overwhelms him. "Can you help me out of here? Out of here, out of here, out of here. Please, can't you help me? I have to get out of here. I have to get out of here, out of here. I need to get out of here. If you could help me get out of here. Please help me get out of here, I need to get out of here, out of here."

Twenty minutes of this, with never a pause.

Only a few days ago I couldn't imagine telling him it was "all right to let go." But now, on his own terms, that's exactly what I say to him: "I'll help you if I can, Dad. I'll help, and you can do it. I know you can do it. You can get out whenever you want, and I'm going to help you."

I'm going to help by giving him as little to eat or drink as I can. In a whole year he hasn't made as many requests as in the last twenty minutes. I *can* help him. I only wish I'd started days ago.

Hours go by in which he says almost nothing, and when he does speak his words are often garbled. But this afternoon, after I give him a pill, he asks with complete lucidity, "What did you put in my mouth?"

"Just a pill," I say. "Something to make you feel better."

I'm aware of the evasion, and so is my father. "What pill?" he asks.

"It's oxycodone," I tell him. "It's a pain reliever."

The name of the drug slows him down. If he once knew what oxycodone was, I'm sure he doesn't now. But I feel caught out anyway, as if I've tried to sneak something over on him. If he's in pain I want to relieve it, but I'm also aware of how easy it is for me, when he's restless and bothersome, when he inches and slides his way down the bed until his feet hang out in the air and he starts his litany again, to just slip him some more oxycodone.

It's a powerful drug with a strong potential for addiction. In my father's case this isn't a problem, but I can't escape the feeling that I'm giving it to him to tranquilize him. So far it has calmed him down every time, because after every dose he goes to sleep. Maybe he can sleep because his pain has been soothed—or perhaps it's because he's so zonked it holds his dementia in check.

There is also my own shady response to narcotics, a few of which I've tried for recreation. Percocet contains oxycodone, and I once swallowed a couple of those to see what kind of buzz they'd give. Appreciable, as I recall. These days I'm well past temptation, because anything half as much fun is likely to trigger a migraine. If I can live without coffee, chocolate, alcohol, cheese, bacon, and anything with maltodextrin, soy protein isolate or "natural flavors"—read MSG—I can do without the surefire headache trigger of marijuana or narcotics. So the little bottle of oxycodone is safe—but I bring to it my own ambivalence.

I'm sure that Alzheimer's patients are drugged all the time when they're too obstreperous. But I'd like to be more inventive. Yesterday when Dad begged me to help him, I told him I would, that we could do it together. I took one leg and began to pull him toward me at the foot of the bed—not enough to actually move him, but stretching out his leg and rocking him forward and back. His legs were so rigid that I could wedge one of them against my hip and pull on the other, stretching without moving him. Ten minutes of that, and a little massage of his knees and ankles, and his mania to get out of here subsided.

But I can't always come up with such an easy distraction. A few days ago I picked up his wallet and led him through a small exploration, pulling out his license, his original Social Security card and his twenty-four dollars. But a day later when I tried to repeat the trick he said, "I know about that," and paid no attention to the wallet. What works every time is the oxycodone.

Another long stretch of agitation with the same refrain: he has to get out of here. He pleads, he begs, he even shouts at Jerry, "No, *now!*"

Together Jerry and I get him into his wheelchair and move him around the house, wherever he wants to go. But nothing soothes him. When we wheel him out of his bedroom he wants to go back in. No, he doesn't want to go outside. No, not to the sunroom. He just wants to get out of here.

Later I massage his legs, and tug on them, and bring him some ginger ale. Advancing his schedule, I give him a half-tablet of oxycodone. I slip it between his lips, as I always do—but before I can get a straw to him he chews the tablet. Then he will take no water at all. He clamps the straw between his teeth, biting down on it hard.

He begs for help. "Do something with me. Please do something with me. I've got to get out of here. Please, it's too much. Let me get out of here, let me get out of here, let me get through here. Do something with me. Take me out of here. Help me get out of here."

He goes on and on. The transcript would fill pages.

When I offer him a pillow he says no. "Take that away from here, take that away, take it away . . . take it away . . . take away . . . taki away, taki away, taki awak . . . taki awakli, taki, taki awakli, taki awaklia. Taki awakli, taki awaklia, taki awaglia, awaglia, taki awaglia, aglia, awaglia, aglia, aglia, aglia, aglia." Then the continuous keening of this new word, *aglia, aglia, aglia, aglia.*

I go upstairs. I have to do something physical, so I start tearing out some old carpet. Over the monitor, *aglia, aglia, aglia,*

aglia. Then some telltale scurrying sounds. I run down and find his legs twenty inches off the end of the bed and headed for the floor. Over his protests I pull him back and push the foot of his bed against the wall, trapping him on the mattress. Unable to escape, he kicks the sheet aside, takes off his underwear, tries to remove his socks. He lifts his skinny legs over the side rails and lets them hang, abrading the skin behind his knees. I pad everything with pillows as he tries to sit up, almost makes it, falls back again.

It's a beautiful day, almost seventy degrees, with the afternoon sun slanting in at a dramatic low angle. I open the wooden sash and the storm window beside his bed, and a light breeze pours in, with the smell of leaves on the ground, the songs of chickadees and thrushes. Dad takes a glance outside, a single three-second glance at the world. Then he's done with it.

From Santa Fe, Lois sends me a copy of a letter she wrote to her brother Steve, who's dying of cancer. "The sun is rising right now, turning the sky a beautiful seashell-pink color in the east. Our apple tree is covered in bright yellow leaves, and the air is mild, about forty-five, and bound to warm up to the sixties by mid-afternoon. What a beautiful world. In spite of all the losses to come, and all the pain of change, I'm still in love with it. The Navajos say, 'With beauty before me, I walk. With beauty behind me, I walk. With beauty below me, I walk. With beauty all around me, I walk.'"

A bad night. I go to bed in the living room at ten, but wake at 12:30 with what I know immediately is a dangerous headache. I take an Imitrex, but it's too late. Go back to sleep, wake around three, give Dad his oxycodone and take my rescue medication, Fiorinal with codeine. No sleep for me after that, because the Fiorinal is loaded with caffeine. Also, it beats the living daylights out of my stomach. At five in the morning I send Al an e-mail describing Dad's condition and my own. "Everyone," I write, "is now drugged and fucked up over here."

Dad stirs at six. I resist getting up until six-thirty, then find his underwear off and shit everywhere. He has dug around with his hand and spread it over the bed rails and sheets, a real mess. After a long cleanup I take everything soiled to the washer—and come back to find another round of shit on the pads and sheets I've just replaced. Headache or no, there's nothing for it but to do the entire cleanup again.

We're starting Dad on a new drug, half a milligram of Ativan, for anxiety, and we'll alternate it with the oxycodone. So far so good. Forty minutes into the first one and he's snoring lightly, his mania at bay. He still moves around a little, but he looks peaceful, which is what I want for him now.

My father lies in bed, naked except for an unbuttoned shirt, his shoulder and head jammed against one of the rails. Mostly he sleeps. As Lois says, "It takes a lot of rest to die." Dad's always drugged now, but at times still moans: "Aglia, aglia, aglia, aglia. I've got to get out of here, I need to go home. Let me go home, please, let me go back, I need to go home."

I tell him he can go whenever he wants. I tell him he's been a great father to me and Al and Joe, and he can go home at any time. He shows no sign that he's heard me, but they say hearing is the last sense to go, so I keep talking to him.

He's on another new medication as well, Levsin, to control the rattling in his throat. It's not exactly a death rattle, because he's not at the edge of dying. It's a deep sonorous liquid gargle, and the new drug alleviates it. The sound was a shock at first, but I was getting used to it. I've had doubts about treating it, having read what the American Geriatrics Society has to say about it: "This noise is not correlated with patient distress but it is disturbing to the family." In other words, Dad is being given the Levsin so I can relax. I think about resisting Hospice on this but yield to their program. The truth is that if he kept up that gargle for hours, I might be desperate to get away from it.

Even scrunched against the side of his bed, Dad looks pretty good. His cheeks are smooth after a shave by Jerry, and his skin color healthy. But he can hardly move. He rarely speaks now, drinks about an ounce of liquid a day, and eats only the ice cream I use to get down his crushed medications. His voice has sunk to a grumble and his sleep apnea is more pronounced, especially under the influence of the oxycodone. He can lie completely still for twenty or thirty seconds at a time, then catch his breath with a hard gasp and a rise of his chest. A dozen times a day I stop at his door to make sure he's still alive.

He may speak or not, he may be approaching death, yet it is always my father lying on that bed. His body falls away but his essential nature hasn't changed, and there is something appealing about him, about his face, about his expression. It's my own sense, I think, that here is someone who has never put up a front, who doesn't need to project an image. Dad is reserved. He has long contained his feelings—but that's him, that's the person he believes in. I, or anyone else, am free to spill my emotions all over the place. I can do whatever crazy thing I want, and all Dad asks is that I let him be himself. After my recent weeks of holding and rubbing him, I see that probably I could have been doing this all year, because if that were my choice he wouldn't have fought it. With all his reserve, my father has been more at ease with himself and how he feels than my mother ever was. She was the secretive parent, the luminous hider. Dad never wanted to roll around in emotional talk. He didn't like it, didn't believe in it and didn't do it—even as he let the rest of us choose our own lives. *Born to serve,* as Al and I used to say, and now I can see how much of himself he gave so that my mother and brother and I could do what we felt like.

Upstairs, I wake in the early morning dark. For a moment I hold onto a dream about my childhood dog, the most comforting dream—then think, *Dad*. But it's not my night to worry about him. It's my night off and I'm lying in bed with the monitor turned down, and I've had a full night's sleep. Even when I reach over and turn the monitor up I can't hear him, the sound of his breathing drowned out by the humidifier and by the pump on his air mattress, installed to help with his bedsore by varying the pressure beneath him. And now, not hearing him, I know I'm finished with sleeping upstairs. I go down and tell the night sitter I won't be needing any more help. My father is dying, and I'm going to move into the living room and stay there, because if he starts to go I don't want one of the sitters to be here in the house. I don't want anyone here, not even Harriet, maybe not even Al. Of course I'll call him, and Joe in Virginia—but what I really want is to be alone with my father when he dies.

As Jerry says, "You want to make God laugh? Just tell him your plans." Yet when I imagine my father's death, there are only the two of us in this quiet house. Many have helped care for him in the last year, but I want his death to myself.

Dad wakes in the night, saying "Jane? Jane? I have to go to work."

After a pause he gets rolling. "I have to go to New York. I have to get out of the house. I have to go across the street. Jane? I have to get out of here." He speaks whole sentences, calmly, with nouns.

Sunday morning. The day begins with light, with quiet, then a blazing sun. I'm not going to tennis and no one is coming over, so my father and I will be alone. I lie on the living room bed, slow to get up, thinking of some quiet days like this during the first week of my son's life.

Clarisa and I were living in southern Chile in a borrowed house, a tiny place with only a bed and two stools for furniture. In those first days home from the hospital, Janir slept as much as my father does now. The sunlight poured in, we lay on the sheets, there was nothing but our small, intoxicating new life together. I made tea on a little gas ring, then eggs and toast. Janir gurgled and waved his arms, a miracle every minute. The morning passed into afternoon, the day into night, and we stayed indoors. After her episiotomy it was a week before Clarisa could walk with any comfort, and only then did we leave the house together.

First we showed Janir off to the neighbors, then walked across a pasture toward a grove of pines. Inside the small forest, Clarisa set Janir down in his blanket on a bed of old needles. He lay there in silence, his round eyes blinking at the boughs overhead. Clarisa took my hand and led me farther into the woods. Fifty feet, a hundred, until the small white blanket was dwarfed. Then we walked back, exclaiming *Mira, mira, es un niño, es un infante.* We knelt on either side of him as if we'd stumbled across a foundling. *Que crées, lo llevamos a casa? Que bello el niño, que perfecto. Mira a esa boca, a los ojos. Es milagro, no crées?*

That was early spring, and this is late fall—but sitting beside my father in his bed, I feel some of that same peace and intoxication. Dad sleeps: *que bello es, que perfecto.* His face has grown smoother and his hair stands up in a nimbus. Though he'd scarcely take notice of it, I'd like to move his bed into a grove of trees.

When choosing a path, said Don Juan, Carlos Castaneda's shaman, ask yourself one question: "Does this path have a heart? If it does, the path is good. If it doesn't, it is of no use." After almost a year at my dad's, I know I have chosen the right path. If I'd stayed in Ohio I could have had my freedom— but I'd have missed this year I've shared with my father, and all that I've learned about the two of us. I've done what I could not do later. And I can see now how happy I've been. Even in these hard final days I've been happy. This is not quite the right word, but almost. "All paths are the same," says Don Juan, "they lead nowhere . . . but one has a heart, the other doesn't. One makes for a joyful journey; as long as you follow it, you are one with it." All year I've been one with my father. Of course I've been sad at times, even miserable when he was miserable, but not once have I been depressed. I've been engaged, I've been involved, and that is happiness to me.

Distance, uninvolvement, reserve: these are my enemies. I probably learned them from my father, with some help from the world at large. And now, ironically, he's the one who has connected me to the rest of the world. I remember moving into his house, how afraid I was of living under the same roof with someone, afraid of being trapped. I'm far beyond that now. I've been consumed by my dad's life, and now I'm consumed by his death. It's coming, and I'll be here.

Late in the morning he stirs. I go in and change the pad beneath him, on which he has dribbled a strong-smelling, tea-colored urine. He doesn't want to wear his Depends, so I let him go without underwear and clean up the sheets when I have to. Days have passed since his last bowel movement, so maybe we're done with that. Now, because I was late with his medications, he's unhappy but talks more. He complains loudly as I roll him from side to side, he speaks whole sentences, he tells me to leave him alone, not to poke him, not to touch him.

"Just *stop* it. Oh Jane, don't *do* that. No, no, no, just leave me alone." When I roll him to get at the damp pad below, he cries out like a child, a pitiable cry, "That *hurts.*"

I blast him with more Ativan, more oxycodone, more Levsin. Before they take effect he grows restless and agitated. "I want to get out of here."

"You're doing a great job, Dad. I think you can get out whenever you want."

"No, I want to get out *tonight*."

"Maybe it will be tonight."

"I want to be *out* of here."

With nothing more to eat or drink, I know he can't last long. But I could do more. I could open up some of those Nembutals and mix them into ice cream and help him die now. That's what he wants, it could not be any clearer. If we were truly alone in our world, I'd do it. But I don't have the nerve. I'm afraid of being caught, afraid of an autopsy, afraid of what my brothers would think. Al has already told me he couldn't do it himself.

If only Dad could ask me. If he said "Give me the Nembutals," I would. But he's far from remembering those pills or any plans he had for them.

Betsy, the Hospice nurse filling in for Deb, came over this afternoon and we talked in the sunroom. I was surprised to hear she thought Dad might last another week or more. A week of misery and hard breathing. "What about the morphine?" I asked her.

"We could start that. Perhaps it's time."

She retrieved it from the Hospice pack in the refrigerator. It comes as a liquid in a small bottle with a dropper: a quarter of a milliliter to start, and I can use it on top of the other drugs.

Changing Dad's bedclothes has become a painful ordeal. Instead of rolling from side to side to help out, as he used to, he now grips the bed rails or the sheets, moaning and refusing to move. So after dinner I drop the first dose of morphine into his open mouth, flush it down with water from a straw, and wait. His hard breaths continue, each coming with a sharp contraction of his belly and diaphragm, then a snort and a wheeze.

Thirty minutes later I change his bedclothes without the least whimper. Already I can see how the morphine takes him deeper than the other drugs, further from pain. But his terrible breathing continues unabated, the jerk of his belly and the hard rasp. I spray him with a decongestant but it seems to have no effect.

I call Al. I call Joe. I tell them what the nurse said about another week, but that Dad seems much worse than that to me.

I sit beside him until ten at night, then crawl into bed and lie there listening to the grind of his breaths. I drift off for a time, then it's midnight and he's moving around in his bed. I get up, give him some more oxycodone and wait, sitting beside him in the darkened room.

An hour of misery. His breaths tear at his body, twenty to the minute, each sounding like it could be his last. Even when apnea stills his lungs, his stomach keeps clenching in the same three-second rhythm.

Another half hour. I drop in .25 milliliters of morphine, and still no change. His body looks inert—at one point his arm falls away from the bed, between the rails, and hangs limp in the air. I tuck it back in and put up another pillow. His agonizing breaths continue.

The tension in the room—my own tension—keeps mounting. I go upstairs, pull out one of the prescription bottles from the bag of Nembutals and take it back to Dad's room. It was prescribed on 10/23/99, is labeled Nembutal 100MG, 30 CAP, and when I spill the tiny yellow wave of capsules onto the bed there are exactly thirty of them. The sight of them comforts me, the way a gun in a drawer might comfort a tormented soul: just to know there's a way out. I'm thinking about it again, thinking I should do this.

Finally, at two in the morning, I can stand it no more and call the Hospice operator. In ten minutes a nurse calls back, and I go over with her all Dad's recent medications. Then I put the phone close to his mouth and let her listen to the spasms of his breathing.

She has me check his hands and feet, all of which are warm. She asks, "What's his face look like?"

In the dim light of the room, sitting in a chair at the side of his bed, I haven't really inspected his face. He has jammed himself into a corner with his neck arched back against a pillow—but when I turn on a light and hover over him I'm surprised to see how peaceful his expression is, how composed and slack. I describe this to the nurse, and tell her how his arm flopped out between the rails.

"I don't think he's in pain," she says. "It sounds to me like end-stage breathing."

"Is this normal? This sound?"

"I've heard a lot worse. I think you're giving him every medication you should. I could send a nurse around tonight—but there's really no reason. If the oxycodone is too hard to administer, just use more morphine."

I thank her, put the Nembutals away and go to bed. I sleep.

Nov 22nd.

Labored breathing all day. Every half hour or so I step into Dad's room and find his face still relaxed and his position in bed unchanged. A dose of morphine in the morning, another at noon. I pull back the sheet to see if he needs to be cleaned up, but he's dry. I think his kidneys are shutting down. All I can do is stand beside him and listen to him breathe. It may not be painful to him, but the dry rasp of it still sounds like agony and tears through my own body.

I feel I should stay beside his bed, that I should be here night and day. In movies or novels, there's always some family member who keeps a constant vigil until the moment of death. I don't. Days have gone by with my father in bed, weeks already, and I get bored in his room. I run out of thoughts and of things to say. I take a cue from Harriet and tell him how nice and warm his feet are, how great he looks and what a good rest he's having. I talk about his grandchildren, I talk about the weather. Then I don't know what to say and go upstairs to paint the floor. There I listen to him over the monitor, his murderous breathing.

No one wants to wind up like this, and I don't believe I will. It's a persistent illusion. Somehow, I think, I'll avoid this disaster. I'll have my Nembutal plans more in line, and will never let this happen. I tell my friends, as many have said themselves, "Shoot me. Don't let me get to that stage." But I know my father would have said the same, and here he is, trapped.

I come down to check on him, I shower, I dribble another dose of morphine into his wide-open mouth. I cook and eat my dinner. After washing the dishes I make a cup of decaf and settle down on a chair beside him. His hands lie on his waist, on top of a sheet embroidered by my grandmother with a band of little pine trees. Some nights I bring in the newspaper and read in silence, but tonight I find things to say. Though it's hard to imagine that he's conscious enough to understand, I talk to him anyway.

"Al is coming down on Friday," I say. "He's going to have Thanksgiving dinner with his family, and the next day he'll drive down and we'll have a good visit with him. I talked with Joe today, too. He and Frances are getting ready for their next baby. I think she could be born any day now. You're going to be quite the grandfather, Dad. You're the first Thorndike with a granddaughter in a hundred and forty years, and now you're going to have two of them."

He doesn't move, he doesn't say anything, his expression doesn't change at all. But I go on. A memory surfaces from my own childhood in Connecticut, something I haven't thought about for years. "Do you remember that doughnut shop in Fairfield? You used to take us over there on Sunday mornings, just Alan and me. I don't remember Mom ever coming along. Most of the doughnuts were made in back, but they had a machine out in front of the counters where you could watch the dough ooze out of a tube and plop down into a vat of boiling oil. The oil had a current that moved the doughnut along, and halfway around it floated onto a little paddle that flipped it over, and then the other side got cooked, and then it was flipped into a hopper. We never got tired of watching that.

"And the bowling alley. Remember that place in Norwalk where they had the smaller balls for kids? It must have been back before they invented pin-setting machines, because there were boys who did the job by hand, scruffy-looking teenagers, maybe even younger. They'd drop down into the pits from above, and set the pins and climb up out of the way so we could roll the next frame. I think I was still figuring out that we had money and some people didn't. We'd drive over there in that old forty-eight Merc of ours, and Alan and I would bowl, but some kids on their Saturday afternoons had to work in the gloom of the pits.

"And that beautiful Mercury convertible. That was a great car. Remember the Quiet Light? You had that made for Mom, because she hated people who honked. If someone honked behind her, she could flip a switch and the big stenciled light would say QUIET, QUIET. Of course, once people saw that they loved it and honked all the time."

Eventually I run out of memories. I've already told him what a great dad he's been, and don't tell him again. I just sit beside his silent form, in the warm room with all the sounds that accompany his breathing: the electric heater, the humidifier, the pump on his mattress, the rumbling of the basement furnace.

This is surely a death watch, but without the leave-taking. There's no grappling with unfinished business, no final resolution. There's just an old man lying in bed, breathing hard, and his son calling up the treasured days of his youth.

At eight o'clock I go out into the living room and work up a lease for a tenant. Then I get up and check again on my father. His breathing is steady, his hands and feet are still warm, his face is tilted back but softened by the morphine. I sit down by his bed and listen to him breathe. It's dark outside. Dad lies in the exact same position I put him in last night when I gave him his medications. His hands are darker and have curled in. His feet are still warm, though swollen. He breathes, and that's all he does. That's his life now. He doesn't eat or drink or say anything.

I can't settle down. I make another cup of decaf, I clear some papers from the dining room table. I don't know what to do with myself. Finally I take a movie I borrowed from the library and load it into my laptop. I haven't watched a movie in three months, but now settle into the lift chair with a pair of earphones for the audio, and allow myself to be drawn into a Hollywood world, a Hannibal Lector movie that is mild at the start but sure to turn gruesome later.

From where I sit in the living room I can see my father's face, just above the pillows that I've jammed around the rails of his hospital bed. I glance at him from time to time, but he hasn't moved an inch. The lights are low, nothing has changed, the movie plays—but only fifteen minutes into it I can't sit still. Something calls me to pause the film and set my laptop on the living room bed. I stand up, walk to Dad's door and lean in. I can't see or hear him breathing.

I step up to the bed and he's *not* breathing, and his color looks bad. Already my heart is racing. Maybe it's just his apnea, I think—and even as I watch he takes a breath, a short hard gasp, and I think yes, it's just the apnea and now he'll start breathing again. But he doesn't. Instead, his open mouth begins to close. Even more ghostly, his arms, which have been resting on his stomach, rise into the air and fold over each other as if to embrace himself. Then they stop, reverse, and settle back. I put one hand on his neck and the other on his chest. He's wearing a plaid shirt split up the back, and through the thin cotton I can feel his heart pounding furiously, far too fast, a hundred and fifty beats a minute, a hundred and eighty: *bam bam bam bam bam bam bam bam bam bam bam.*

Then it stops.

His heart has stopped and he's not breathing. This is death, but I don't see anything. Friends have told me I would see his soul depart, that it would be obvious, that it would lift off in a rush of intense quivering energy. I don't believe in a soul that survives and goes elsewhere, but I want to see it anyway. I stare at Dad's face, now perfectly still. He's dead. My hands still rest on his chest and neck. I watch his lips and the pale skin of his nostrils—but I'm aware of things I don't want to be thinking about: my laptop still running in the living room, and all the sounds in his bedroom. I duck out to my computer and press the power button, then come back and turn off the humidifier, the electric heater, and the pump on the air mattress. It takes only twenty seconds, and now I can be present in the quiet room. But in those seconds death eludes me. I stare again at my father's face. I've let myself be distracted, I've come back to someone who looks no different than he did an hour ago. I keep trying to get back to the shock of feeling his heart stop under my palm. I touch his forehead, his hands and bare feet. He's warm all over—which leads me to worry that I've made a mistake, that in fact he isn't dead. But he is. I go around to the other side of the bed where there's more room, climb over the rails and lie down beside him, and immediately start to cry.

After only a minute I stop. I feel self-conscious. I keep thinking Dad will look over and see me weeping, and it will make him uncomfortable. I take one of his hands in mine, and he lets me do it. Of course he lets me. I lie beside him and watch the pale skin of his forehead. I'm still trying to get his death into me, and still it escapes me. His eyes are closed, his face at rest, his shoulders settled into the pillow. The morphine calmed him, and I wonder if it killed him. I slide one hand around the back of his neck and hold the other around his chest, so that he's fully in my arms. Now that he's dead I'm holding him as I never could in life—and it's that thought that pitches me into the deepest sobbing, loud and shameless.

I lie beside him for almost an hour, then get up to call Al and Joe and describe his death to them. I stand in the kitchen, not wanting to talk about Dad within earshot of him, and wind up almost whispering. Al can't believe I'm going to pass the night with his body in the next room, but I don't want to call Hospice now and have someone come over and pronounce him dead. I don't want to put on some kind of face, and rise to the occasion, and worry about other people's reactions. I just want to be with him. Hospice can come in the morning. I'll call Harriet then, and Janir, and Jane's daughter Susie and several others. Al will drive down to see him before the funeral home takes him away.

By now it's eleven-thirty at night. I move around my father's room, gathering up his medications, his lotions and extra bed pads. Every few minutes I stop to feel his forehead, then his chest. I keep checking on him to make sure he's dead. He is, but it's hard to take in. I have to feel his feet and hands, make sure again that he's not breathing. I'm glad no one else is here, but by midnight I'm far from sleep. I'm restless. I clear the coffee table, I pile up the newspapers and magazines and close my laptop. I wanted to be alone with my father, to know death, to cry—but now something is making me anxious and I can't sit still.

I put on a coat. I'll walk to the Island Pond Cemetery and stand where half his ashes will be buried. On the lawn I pause, imagining the shock if someone were to go into the house and find him. But no one has ever come over at this hour, and I set off down the empty bike path. It's cold. The cemetery, only ten minutes away, is wooded and hilly and filled with winding drives and pathways. From branches above the graves several families have hung chimes, which now ring in the gusty dark. Last winter I cross-country skied here, last spring I came for the lilacs, and in the summer two ducks lived on the pond only yards from my dad's plot. All those times my dad was alive, and now he isn't. I hold my hand to my chest to feel my own heart, but it doesn't help me settle down. It's walking that calms me, so I leave the pond behind and wander through the cemetery, up and down the lanes past the dark tombstones.

At home nothing has changed. Chilled after my walk, I take off my shoes, climb back in bed with my father, and pull his pine-tree-embroidered sheet up to our chins. His body is warmer than mine, and I feel the heat coming off his chest, covered only by his old plaid shirt. I lie on my back beside him in the quiet room, getting used to the stillness. To the way it will be, now that our long walk together has ended. Over the years we've had our struggles, but through this painful last stretch, as he fought the loss of memory, language, and reason, I've watched him do the best he could. His whole life, it's now clear to me, he has done the same. He did the best he could with my mother, with me and my brothers, with his second wife Margery and his great and good friend Jane. I've watched this, I've seen it all before—but now, lying shoulder to shoulder with him on his narrow bed, the certainty of it seeps into my body.

Slowly, even as he cools, I warm up under the sheet. I sink back, I close my eyes in the silent house. I lie there so long I almost fall asleep—until I snap to with a jerk, afraid of how strange it would feel to wake up beside him. I climb out onto the floor and tug him into the center of the bed, then pick out his traveling clothes for tomorrow and lay them over his feet: a pair of khakis and a newer plaid shirt.

Still, I'm restless. I stand at the window and look out at Oak Street, shining faintly under the streetlights. I want to keep moving, I want to go to the ocean. I put on a warmer coat, leave my father once again and drive to Nauset Heights the back way, never passing another car. I park as I would in August, in the McGees' grassy yard. All around me the dark summer houses are empty, looming behind bare hedges as I walk to the landing above the stairs. Somewhere there's a moon, but clouds blanket the sky. There's just enough light to show the long sweep of sandy shoreline, with the darker water beyond. I'm glad to be moving. I can hear the waves, then smell them, as I make my way down the stairs, holding onto the splintery railing.

From the base of the dunes to the water, a recent storm has swept the beach. The wind blows a hole in the clouds and for thirty seconds the moonlight shows through, exposing a wide strip of planed sand with no tire tracks, no sand castles, no abrupt shelving, only a few long strands of seaweed. I cross the beach and stop at the edge of the continent, facing the sea and the raw wind—until a big wave hisses up out of the dark and sends me running. I return and keep an eye out for the next one. Hunched in my coat, I try to imagine the summer evening on which we'll throw the last of my father's ashes into the ocean. The waves keep streaming in. Every few seconds they come, every minute of every day, in a beat as steady as my dad's heart.

Two Years Later

Two years after my father dies, LL gives birth to a son, Maximo Holst Thorndike, and Janir sends me this description of their first days:

We lie there with him.
We kiss him all over.
We put his feet in our mouths.
I kiss his tongue and gums.
He sleeps on my chest.
He likes to be swaddled.
He likes to be in a fetal position, if we pull
    out his arms or feet he pulls them back in.
LL feeds him, we burp him, and sometimes
    we just let him lie there being a baby.

"I can't get enough," Janir writes. "I want to wear him somehow. I want to wrap a blanket of Maximo around me."

His exuberance reminds me of my dad's joy—his near delirium—at playing with his grand-daughter. No wonder I study my parents. Within the compass of their lives everything is foretold.

When Max is eight weeks old I fly out to Colorado to meet him. Though his day-of-birth photos showed him scrunched up and red, when LL brings him to the airport he's smooth and brown and gorgeous. I take him in my arms as he sleeps, careful of his head and neck. I don't have the confidence I had with Janir at this age. Since then I've held many babies, but none this young.

My nephew Ted is here for a visit, and at home there are four of us kissing Max. All day, whether he's asleep or awake, someone is kissing him, caressing his head, making faces at him, or rocking him in their arms.

A couple of days later, as I sit on the couch beside him, LL comes over, kneels on the floor and hovers above him, kissing his little mouth, his nose, his eyebrows, and courting his elusive smile. "I just want to eat him," she says, "so I can have him back inside me." Not in the womb—she had enough of that by the time he was born—but within her, all through her, an irreducible part of her.

When Janir comes home from work it's the same story. He coos over his sleeping son, gives him kisses and more kisses. I haven't been ignoring Max, but reading a book as I sit beside him. Janir nuzzles him, holds his face close, breathes him in, kisses his chin. After ten minutes of this he stands up and says, "You don't like babies as much as I do, do you Dad?"

I have to laugh. "I don't see how I could. But there was a time."

Early the next morning I'm lying in bed reading after a good night's sleep. I've heard Max's cries a couple of times, but I'm not the one who's been up half the night feeding him and changing his diapers. At seven Janir knocks on my door, turns the knob and comes in. He looks like he's been hit by a truck. He holds Max out in his blue nightsuit and says *Take him.* So we can sleep."

Max fusses. He lies on my chest, moving his head from one side to the other, his new trick, but he won't settle down. He isn't cold, he isn't wet, so maybe he's hungry. I get up and fix him two ounces of formula—he gets breast milk and formula, both—then burp him, then give him another two ounces. Still he groans a little, and his forehead is fluted where his tiny brows meet. It's been thirty-seven years since I lay around with an infant. What does Max want? What keeps his brows from relaxing? Usually just lying on his father's chest, or mine, is enough to quiet him down, but not now.

I let him squiggle around, helping him a little as he slides half off my chest into the crook of my arm. With his body pointing downhill he looks more peaceful. He turns toward me as he goes to sleep, his brow smooths out, and for thirty minutes I watch his radiant face. God, what beauty. The weight of him in my arms, the peace of it, the purest love on earth—it all comes gliding back. We're all going to love him, and Max can live in our attention. I keep holding him. I watch him breathe, I kiss his little fingers and think, *This is what I've done with* my *life.*

In August we're all back on Cape Cod for our family reunion: days of volleyball and kayaking, and early evening dinners at the beach in the last of the soft Cape light. One quiet afternoon I take Max out in his stroller, pushing him down the bike bath where I used to roll my dad in his wheelchair. He's quiet. We pass the tennis courts and the blue water tower, and I keep thinking he's going to fall asleep. But he doesn't: every time I bend forward for a look, he's staring out at the world. In the house he often gets bored—the same old toys, the same old sights—but outside he watches everything with deep attention.

After a quarter mile in one direction we turn around and head back past the house, toward the cemetery. It's lush after a wet summer. There are flowers in bloom and American flags, birdhouses on posts and silent chimes. I wheel Max past weathered nineteenth-century tombstones, past a man lost at sea, past a girl who died in her seventeenth year. I know these stones from earlier walks and explain them to Max as we pass by. He's as watchful as ever, staring up into the trees with what Janir calls his *someday-I'm-going-to-get-there* look. His head tilts to one side, but he doesn't go to sleep. We come to the pond, where I wheel him over the grass and park him directly over my father's flat granite stone.

Joseph J. Thorndike

1913–2005

Max stares at the pond and its splashing fountain. He stares at the light as it plays through the leaves overhead. I sit down beside him, rest a hand on my dad's stone and let my temple graze against my grandson's. From below us, as if welling out of the ground, I can feel my father's presence: his ambition, his knowledge, his failures, his devotion. All this I will share with Max, so my dad will not be lost.